OPPRESSIVE
LIGHT

OPPRESSIVE LIGHT

SELECTED POEMS BY
ROBERT WALSER

Translated and Edited by
Daniele Pantano

BLACK LAWRENCE PRESS

CONTENTS

For Nicole, Fiona, and Giacomo.

For James Reidel.

And for Thomas "T-Man" Daniel Leavines.

—DP

INTRODUCTION

To paraphrase Musil's famous aphorism regarding Reason, the path of Robert Walser's poetry "is the path of a cloud" in the rarified air of a solitary life, adrift in an evil century, moving with the lightness of an accomplished soul. One enters his language to be enveloped in gentle agonies, dark praise, rays of bright pleasure and the tumult of recognitions regarding selfhood and the fog of self, an *ich ohne ich*. This lyric cloud forms at the beginning of his writing life, with the earliest poem "Im Bureau," wherein the poet, as a "miserable clerk," is "made humble," his language floating across the moon, a "wound of night."

As a young man, Walser left his birthplace of Biel/Bienne, Switzerland, for Stuttgart, Germany, where, having failed his first audition as an actor, he resolved to become a poet, earning his living as a clerk moving from job to job before returning to Switzerland, on foot, to continue in clerical positions. After fulfilling his military obligations, he entered the employ of a failed inventor, and then trained as a servant, working as a butler in a castle in Upper Silesia. In 1905, he moved to Berlin to join his brother, a painter of theater sets, and here, living frugally in rooming houses, he wrote his first three masterful novels, as well as short stories, sketches, 'dramolets' and feuilletons popular in magazines and newspapers of the day. He was accepted in literary circles and admired by Franz Kafka, Robert Musil and also Walter Benjamin, who wrote that in Walser's sentences, "the idea that stumbles around . . . is a thief, a vagabond and a genius." In these years, prose flowed fluently from his pen, in a script that was nearly calligraphic in its execution. The flâneur, the servant, the poet and salaried clerk moved as characters through his dreamscapes, anonymous and evanescent. His sentences seemed to cascade and vanish like veils of falling water upon rock. The late W. G. Sebald thought that Walser shared Gogol's secret of "utter superfluity . . . the awful provisionality of their respective existences, the prismatic mood swings, the sense of panic, the wonderfully capricious humor steeped at the same time in blackest heartache, the endless scraps of paper and, of course, the invention of a whole populace of lost souls, a ceaseless masquerade for the purpose of autobiographical mystification."

Walser's life swerves here, through a return to Switzerland, military service, the loss of his father, a brother's suicide, periods of prodigious writing and self-disparagement, poverty and isolation, and finally the closing of his "little prose-piece workshop." A crippling cramp in his writing hand forced him then to invent what he called "the pencil method,"—writing in pencil on paper scraps, in a miniscule and, for years, indecipherable hand of "tiny, antlike markings" that his friend, Carl Seelig, assumed was a secret code.

The sequence is unclear to me, but it seems that after periods of drinking and depression, his sister urged him to enter a mental sanatorium in Waldau, and although doctors couldn't agree on a diagnosis, finally settling on schizophrenia, he would live incarcerated in mental hospitals in Waldau and later Herisau for a quarter of a century, until his death. He spent his days at menial tasks such as sorting beans and making paper bags; he read magazines and took long walks, especially at night. He declined a room of his own, choosing to sleep in the asylum barracks. Although he showed no outward signs of mental illness, he refused to live in the world again, and when asked by a visitor about his writing, he famously answered: "I'm not here to write, I'm here to be mad."

The later poems are dated from 1924 to 1933, spanning the years of his confinement. The last of them had to have been written "from the pencil area," a provisional *brouillon* of light drafts that freed his hand and didn't at all resemble his past experience of sitting "for hours bent over a single word that has to take the long slow route from brain to paper." The penciled script allowed him, according to J. M. Coetzee, "the purposeful, uninterrupted, yet dreamy hand movement that had become indispensable to his creative mood." In the asylum, he never felt himself to be in a hurry. The asylum walls and also his long walks on the grounds and beyond afforded him solitude, and in the barracks and wards, he found companionship of the sort he could bear. "I would wish it on no one to be me," he wrote, "Only I am capable of bearing myself. To know so much, to have seen so much, and/ To say nothing, just about nothing."

The late poems include "To Georg Trakl," the Austrian poet who would have been Walser's contemporary, and with whom he shared affinities, lyric and experiential, having to do with literary gifts and mental fragility, who shared a sense of apartness on earth, and who was also hospitalized (in Krakow) for a mental breakdown in the aftermath of attending to ninety wounded soldiers in Galicia whose lives he could not save. Trakl's friend, Ludwig von Ficker, attempted to intercede on his behalf and also preserved his work, just as Walser's friend Carl Seelig would later do. They shared a radiant awareness of nature, the brevity of conscious life, and the instability of selfhood. Of reading Trakl's work, Walser wrote to the poet: "I found myself in the chasm of reading,/ in the pursuit of your being's beauty," and later, "I dedicate this speech, playfully, dreamlike/ to your genius." And in conclusion, "When I read your poems/ I feel as if/ I'm being driven away by a magnificent chaise."

Throughout the poems, early and late, we find the vocation announced, to which Walser would devote his life: the spiritual and later corporeal work of vanishing from the world. This is everywhere available in the lyrics: "They abandoned me, so I learned to forget myself/ which allowed me to bathe in my inspired soul." And later in the same poem: "Because they didn't want to know me, I became self-aware." In another he is "enchanted/ by the idea that I've been forgotten." Of the place in which he has vanished, he writes "I only know that it's quiet here,/ stripped of all needs and doings,/ here it feels good, here I can rest,/ for no time measures my time." With untold suffering behind him perhaps, in the interstices of his recorded life, he seems to write his way toward a liminal state of non-attachment and hovering, weightless acceptance: "The world is inside an hour,/ unaware, not needing anything,/ and, oh, I don't always know/ where it rests and sleeps, my world." His world is other-where, and he without it, and we emerge from reading his lyric art as a cloud would disperse in raw light, with unexpected clarity, having followed the poet's footsteps to where he was found on Christmas Day in 1956, lying in the snow, his eyes open, his heart still, with snow on his shoulders and his soul loosed.

—Carolyn Forché
In "October" he advises us to *be glad, be gentle and kind/ and patient.*

October, 2011

"I would wish it on no one to be me.
Only I am capable of bearing myself.
To know so much, to have seen so much, and
To say nothing, just about nothing."

—RW

OPPRESSIVE
LIGHT

From
EARLY LYRICS
(1897-1912)

From
POEMS
(1909)

IM BUREAU

Der Mond blickt zu uns hinein,
er sieht mich als armen Kommis
schmachten unter dem strengen Blick
meines Prinzipals.
Ich kratze verlegen am Hals.
Dauernden Lebenssonnenschein
kannte ich noch nie.
Mangel ist mein Geschick;
kratzen zu müssen am Hals
unter dem Blick des Prinzipals.

Der Mond ist die Wunde der Nacht,
Blutstropfen sind alle Sterne.
Ob ich dem blühenden Glück auch ferne,
ich bin dafür bescheiden gemacht.
Der Mond ist die Wunde der Nacht.

IN THE OFFICE

The moon peers in on us.
He sees me as a miserable clerk
languishing under the strict gaze
of my boss.
Embarrassed, I scratch my neck.
I've never known
life's lasting sunshine.
My flaw is my skill;
having to scratch my neck
under the boss's gaze.

The moon is the wound of night.
Every star is a blood drop.
Though far from the flower of luck,
I'm made humble for it.
The moon is the wound of night.

ABEND (I)

Schwarzgelb im Schnee vor mir leuchtet
ein Weg und geht unter Bäumen her.
Es ist Abend, und schwer
ist die Luft von Farben durchfeuchtet.

Die Bäume, unter denen ich gehe,
haben Äste wie Kinderhände;
sie flehen ohne Ende
unsäglich lieb, wenn ich stille stehe.

Ferne Gärten und Hecken
brennen in dunklem Wirrwarr,
und der glühende Himmel sieht angststarr,
wie die Kinderhände sich strecken.

EVENING (I)

In the snow before me a path glimmers
black-yellow and goes on beneath the trees.
It's evening, and the air is heavy
And damp with colors.

The trees beneath which I walk
have branches like children's hands;
they plead without end,
ineffably kind, when I stand still.

Distant gardens and hedges
burn in a dark mess,
and the glowing sky, rigid with fear,
sees how the children's hands are reaching.

WINTERSONNE

Auf Wänden und an Mauern,
es wird nicht lange dauern,
brennt goldner Sonnenschein.
Der Tag hat aufgehoben,
was auf dem Land gewoben,
was Nacht und Nebel war.
Beruhigendes Lärmen,
Bruststrecken, Händewärmen,
seliger Sonnenschein.
Nun hab' ich auch vergessen,
was lang auf mir gesessen,
was Schmerz und Schwere war.

WINTER SUN

On house and garden walls,
it won't be long,
golden sunshine burning.
Day has lifted
what was woven in the countryside,
what was night and mist.
Reassuring noises,
expanding the chest, rubbing the hands,
blessed sunshine.
I too have now forgotten
what's been weighing on me,
what was pain and suffering.

WARUM AUCH?

Als nun ein solcher klarer
Tag hastig wieder kam,
sprach er voll ruhiger, wahrer
Entschlossenheit langsam:
Nun soll es anders sein,
ich stürze mich in den Kampf hinein;
ich will gleich so vielen andern
aus der Welt tragen helfen das Leid,
will leiden und wandern,
bis das Volk befreit.
Will nie mehr müde mich niederlegen;
es soll etwas
geschehen; da überkam ihn ein Erwägen,
ein Schlummer: ach, laß doch das.

BUT WHY?

Now as such a clear
day came rushing back,
full of calm, true determination,
he spoke slowly:
Now it shall be different,
I'll join the battle;
like so many others,
I want to help rid the world of misery,
want to suffer and walk
until the people are free.
Never again shall I rest my tired head;
something must
happen; then a consideration caught up with him,
a nap: oh, forget it.

DIE BÄUME (I)

(Eine Ballade)

Sie sollten nicht die Fäuste ballen,
meine Sehnsucht ist es, die sich ihnen naht;
nicht so zornerfüllt umherstehen,
meine Sehnsucht naht sich schüchtern ihnen;
nicht wie böse Hunde sprungbereit sein,
als wenn sie meine Sehnsucht zerreißen wollten;
nicht mit weiten Ärmeln drohen,
meiner Sehnsucht tut das weh.
Warum sind sie auf einmal umgewandelt?
Gleich groß und gleich tief ist meine Sehnsucht.
So schwer es ist, so drohend es ist:
ich muß zu ihnen gehn und bin schon da.

THE TREES (I)

(A Ballad)

They should not clench their fists,
it's my longing that's drawing near to them;
they should not stand there full of rage,
my longing is timidly drawing near to them;
they should not be ready to pounce like vicious dogs,
as if they wanted to tear my longing to shreds;
they should not threaten with broad sleeves,
that pains my longing.
Why have they suddenly changed?
As great and deep is my longing.
No matter how difficult, no matter how menacing:
I must reach them and I'm already there.

BRAUSEN

Es braust noch immer in der Welt,
das Brausen hört doch niemals auf;
ich liebe – niemals hört es auf,
es braust ein Lieben durch die Welt.

Und ob ich auch ein Feigling bin
und ob du auch ein Kranker bist:
du liebst, wenn du es auch nicht bist,
der liebt, ich liebe, wenn ich's auch nicht bin.

Es braust, und ich steh' horchend still,
ich weiß, ich hasse den und den,
es nützt mir nichts; wie ich auch will:
ich liebe alles, so auch den.

Dann gibt es Stunden, wo ich weiß,
daß wir vor Liebe alle heiß.

RUSHING

In the world there's still this rush,
the rush that never ceases;
I love—and it will never stop,
a love that rushes through the world.

And even though I'm a coward
and even though you're an invalid:
you love, though it's not you
who loves, I love, though it's not me.

It rushes, and I stand still, listening,
I know I hate this one and that one,
it's no use to me; whatever I intend:
I love everything, so that one, too.

Then there are times when I know
that for love we all burn.

WIE IMMER

Die Lampe ist noch da,
der Tisch ist auch noch da,
und ich bin noch im Zimmer,
und meine Sehnsucht, ah,
seufzt noch wie immer.

Feigheit, bist du noch da?
und, Lüge, auch du?
Ich hör' ein dunkles Ja:
das Unglück ist noch da,
und ich bin noch im Zimmer
wie immer.

AS ALWAYS

The lamp is still here,
the table is also still here,
and I'm still in the room,
and my longing, ah,
still sighs, as always.

Cowardice, are you still here?
and Lie, you, too?
I hear a dim, Yes:
Misfortune is still here,
and I'm still in the room,
as always.

ANGST (I)

Ich möchte,
die Häuser regten sich,
sie kämen auf mich los,
das wäre schauerlich.

Ich möchte,
mein Herz verdrehte sich,
und mein Verstand stünd' still,
das wäre schauerlich.

Das Schauerlichste möchte
ich pressen an mein Herz.
Ich sehne mich nach Angst,
nach Schmerz.

FEAR (I)

I wish
the houses would move,
come after me,
that would be frightening.

I wish
my heart would twist,
and my mind stop,
that would be frightening.

The most frightful I wish to
press against my heart.
I long for fear,
for pain.

SCHÄFERSTUNDE

Hier ist es still, hier bin ich gut,
hier sind die Matten frisch und rein,
und Schattenplatz und Sonnenschein
sind sich wie artige Kinder gut.
Hier ist mein Leben aufgelöst,
das eine harte Sehnsucht ist,
ich weiß nicht mehr, was Sehnsucht ist,
hier ist mein Wollen aufgelöst.
Ich bin so still, so warm bewegt,
es ziehen Linien durchs Gefühl,
ich weiß nicht, alles ist Gewühl,
und doch ist alles widerlegt.
Ich höre keine Klagen mehr,
und doch ist Klage in dem Raum,
so sanfter Art, so weiß, so Traum,
und wieder weiß ich gar nichts mehr.
Ich weiß nur, daß es still hier ist,
entblößt von allem Drang und Tun,
hier bin ich gut, hier kann ich ruhn,
da keine Zeit die Zeit mir mißt.

TRYST

Here it's quiet, here it feels good,
here the meadows are fresh and pure,
and a spot in shade and sunshine
like well-behaved children.
Here the strong desire
that is my life dissolves,
I no longer know desire,
here my will dissolves.
I'm so still, so warmly moved,
lines draw through my emotions,
I don't know, it's all confused,
yet everything's been proven wrong.
I no longer hear any complaints,
yet there's complaining in the room
of such a soft kind, so white, so dreamy,
and again I'm left knowing nothing.
I only know that it's quiet here,
stripped of all needs and doings,
here it feels good, here I can rest,
for no time measures my time.

HEIMKEHR (I)

An meinen Wangen brennt es heiß,
auf meiner Lippe bebt es noch,
weil ich mein Herz ihr übertrug
zum Sprechen; alle Sprache war
voll Irrtum und Befangenheit,
ein Übermut, ein jäher Klang.
So war mein Sprechen, ach, dies zeigt
sich auf der roten Wange noch,
die ich nach Hause trage jetzt.
Ich senke meinen Blick zum Schnee
und geh' vorbei an manchem Haus,
an mancher Hecke, manchem Baum,
der Schnee ziert Hecke, Baum und Haus.
Ich geh' vorbei, den Blick zum Schnee
gesenkt, an meiner Wange ist
nichts, als erinnerungsheißes Rot,
mich mahnend an die wüste Sprach'.

RETURNING HOME (I)

My cheeks are red hot,
my lip still trembles,
because I sent my heart
to speak; every word of it
delusional and awkward,
an exuberance, an abrupt sound.
That's how I spoke, oh, it still
shows on my hot cheeks
I'm now carrying home.
I look down at the snow
and walk past many houses,
past many hedges, many trees,
the snow adorns hedge, tree and house.
I walk on, staring down
at the snow, on my cheeks
nothing but red-hot memory
reminding me of my wild talk.

WEITER

Ich wollte stehen bleiben,
es trieb mich wieder weiter,
vorbei an schwarzen Bäumen,
doch unter schwarzen Bäumen
wollt' ich schnell stehen bleiben,
es trieb mich wieder weiter,
vorbei an grünen Wiesen,
doch an den grünen Wiesen
wollt' ich nur stehen bleiben,
es trieb mich wieder weiter,
vorbei an armen Häuschen,
bei einem dieser Häuschen
möcht' ich doch stehen bleiben,
betrachtend seine Armut,
und wie sein Rauch gemächlich
zum Himmel steigt, ich möchte
jetzt lange stehen bleiben.
Dies sagte ich und lachte,
das Grün der Wiesen lachte
der Rauch stieg räuchlich lächelnd,
es trieb mich wieder weiter.

ONWARDS

I wanted to stop,
I carried onwards,
past black trees,
but under black trees
I already wanted to stop,
I carried onwards,
past green meadows,
but next to those green meadows
I only wanted to stop,
I carried onwards,
past needy little cottages,
beside one of these cottages,
I really would've liked to stop,
to regard its need,
and how the smoke gently
rises into the sky, I would
like to stop now for a while.
That's what I said and laughed,
the green of the meadows laughed
the smoke rose smiling like smoke,
I carried onwards.

SÜNDE

Ich sehe, wie sie leuchten,
die nacht- und morgenfeuchten,
erwärmten Wiesengründe.
Ich seh' die Sonne blenden,
ich sitze zwischen Wänden
und Mauern, es ist Sünde.

Es gehen helle Schatten
durch aufgeregte Matten,
die jetzt ein bunt Getäfel.
Ich sitze so gefangen
in Mißmut und in bangen
Gedanken, es ist Frevel.

SIN

I see how they glow,
the night and morning dews,
the heated meadows.
I see the blinding sun,
I sit among wall after
wall, it's a sin.

Bright shadows
are walking through
unsettled pastures
now colorful panels.
I sit so trapped by anger
and fear, it's a crime.

EIN LANDSCHÄFTCHEN

Dort steht ein Bäumlein im Wiesengrund
und noch viele artige Bäumlein dazu.
Ein Blättlein friert im frostigen Wind
und noch viele einzelne Blättlein dazu.
Ein Häuflein Schnee schimmert an Baches Rand
und noch viele weiße Häuflein dazu.
Ein Spitzlein Berg lacht in den Grund hinein
und noch viele schuftige Spitze dazu.
Und in dem allem der Teufel steht
und noch viele arme Teufel dazu.
Ein Englein kehrt ab sein weinend Gesicht
und alle Engel des Himmels dazu.

A LITTLE LANDSCAPE

There's a little tree in the meadowland
and many more good little trees there too.
A little leaf freezes in the frosty wind
and many lone little leaves there too.
A little pile of snow shimmers at the edge of a brook
and many more little white piles there too.
A small mountain peak laughs into the ground around it
and many more impish peaks there too.
And in the middle of it all stands the Devil
and still more poor devils there too.
A little angel turns away his weeping face
and all heaven's angels there too.

BEISEIT

Ich mache meinen Gang;
der führt ein Stückchen weit
und heim; dann ohne Klang
und Wort bin ich beiseit.

PUT ASIDE

I make my way;
it goes on a bit
towards home; then without a sound,
without a word, I'm put aside.

DRÜCKENDES LICHT

Zwei Bäume stehen im Schnee,
der Himmel, müde des Lichts,
zieht heim, und sonst ist nichts
als Schwermut in der Näh'.

Und hinter den Bäumen ragen
dunkle Häuser hinauf.
Jetzt hört man etwas sagen,
jetzt bellen Hunde auf.

Nun erscheint der liebe, runde
Lampenmond im Haus.
Nun geht das Licht wieder aus,
als klaffte eine Wunde.

Wie klein ist hier das Leben
und wie groß das Nichts.
Der Himmel, müde des Lichts,
hat alles dem Schnee gegeben.

Die zwei Bäume neigen
ihre Köpfe sich zu.
Wolken durchziehn die Ruh'
der Welt im Reigen.

OPPRESSIVE LIGHT

Two trees stand in the snow,
the sky, tired of light,
moves home, and nothing else
but gloom close by.

And behind the trees
dark houses tower up.
Now you hear something said,
now dogs begin to bay.

And the dear, round lamp-
moon appears in the house.
And the light goes out again,
as a wound yawns open.

How small life is here
and how big nothingness.
The sky, tired of light,
has given everything to the snow.

The two trees bow
their heads to each other.
Clouds cross the world's
silence in a circle dance.

BANGEN

Ich habe so lang gewartet auf süße
Töne und Grüße, nur einen Klang.

Nun ist mir bang; nicht Töne und Klingen,
nur Nebel dringen im Überschwang.

Was heimlich sang auf dunkler Lauer:
Versüße mir, Trauer, jetzt schweren Gang.

AFRAID

I've waited so long for sweet
talk and greetings, only one sound.

Now I'm afraid; no talk or sound,
only fog setting in in excess.

Whatever was singing and hiding in the dark:
Misery, sweeten now my grave path.

SEHT IHR

Seht ihr mich über Wiesen ziehn,
die steif und tot vom Nebel sind?
Ich habe Sehnsucht nach dem Heim,
dem Heim, noch nie von mir erreicht,
und auch von einer Hoffnung nicht
berührt, daß ich es jemals kann.
Nach solchem Heim, noch nie berührt,
trag' ich die Sehnsucht, nimmermehr
stirbt sie, wie jene Wiese stirbt,
die steif und tot vom Nebel ist.
Seht ihr mich angstvoll drüber ziehn?

DO YOU SEE?

You do see me crossing the meadow
stiff and dead from the mist?
I long for that home,
that home I've never had,
and without any hope
that I'll ever be able to reach it.
For such a home, never touched,
I carry that longing that will
never die, like that meadow dies
stiff and dead from the mist.
You do see me crossing it, full of dread?

UND GING

Er schwenkte leise seinen Hut
und ging, heißt es vom Wandersmann.
Er riß die Blätter von dem Baum
und ging, heißt es vom rauhen Herbst.
Sie teilte lächelnd Gnaden aus
und ging, heißt's von der Majestät.
Es klopfte nächtlich an die Tür
und ging, heißt es vom Herzeleid.
Er zeigte weinend auf sein Herz
und ging, heißt es vom armen Mann.

AND LEFT

He quietly waved his hat
and left, they say of the wayfarer.
It tore the leaves off the tree
and left, they say of the harsh autumn.
Smiling, she shared her mercy
and left, they say of her Majesty.
At night it knocked on the door
and left, they say of heartbreak.
Crying, he pointed at his heart
and left, they say of the poor man.

STUNDE

Die Stunde kommt, die Stunde geht;
in einer Stunde liegt so viel,
liegt der Gefühle Widerspiel,
liegt Sehnsucht, die wie Frühwind weht.
In einer Stunde spricht der Tag
sein Beten oder Fluchen aus,
und ich bin stets das arme Haus,
gefüllt mit Jubel oder Plag'.
In einer Stunde liegt die Welt
nichtsahnend, nichtsbegehrend so,
und ach, ich weiß nicht immer wo
sie ruht und schlummert, meine Welt.

HOUR

The hour comes, the hour goes;
there's so much in an hour,
the tit-for-tat of emotions,
the longing that blows like a morning breeze.
The day says its prayers
and curses in an hour,
and I'm always the poor house
filled with cheers or laments.
The world lies inside an hour,
unaware, not needing anything,
and, ha, I don't always know
where it rests and sleeps, my world.

From
STRING AND DESIRE
(posthumously published manuscript)

WIESENGRÜN

Hervorgetreten ist
aus hingegangnem Schnee
ein schönes Wiesengrün,
ein Grün, ein dunkles Grün.
Dasselbe scheint der Welt
als milde Sonne jetzt,
als wilde Sonne jetzt,
als warme Sonne jetzt.
Die rechte scheint ja nicht,
die rechte wärmt ja nicht.
Die rechte ist ja weg.
Viel dichte Wolken sind
vor ihrem Glanz, der nun
der Welt auch so nicht fehlt,
weil dunkles Wiesengrün
aus hingegangnem Schnee
als Sonne scheint der Welt.
Als Sonne wärmt die Welt,
als Sonne schmückt die Welt:
hervorgetretnes Grün.

MEADOW GREEN

A lovely meadow
green has emerged
from the melted snow,
a green, a dark green.
The same appears to the world
now as a mild sun,
now as a wild sun,
now as a warm sun.
For the real one doesn't shine,
the real one doesn't warm.
For the real one is gone.
Thick clouds cover
the glow the world
doesn't miss anyway,
because the dark meadow
green from melted snow
appears as a sun to the world.
As a sun it warms the world,
as a sun it adorns the world:
this green that emerged.

ABEND (II)

Nicht nur am Himmel ist
ein weites Abendgrau.
Auch auf der ganzen Welt
ist weites Abendgrau.
Der Schnee ist abendstill.
Das Grün ist abendschön,
die Bäume ebenso,
die Häuser ebenso.
Und von den Häusern weg
steigt Rauch zur Abendluft,
die so voll Glück für mich.
Mein Glück ist Abendglück.

EVENING (II)

The vast evening gray
is not just the sky.
A vast evening gray
covers the entire world.
The snow is silent as evening.
The green is beautiful as evening,
the trees, too,
the houses, too.
And smoke rises from
the houses into evening air
filled with happiness for me.
My happiness is the happiness of evening.

AM FENSTER (II)

Zum Fenster sehe ich
hinaus, es ist so schön,
hinaus, es ist nicht viel.
Es ist ein wenig Schnee,
auf den es regnet jetzt.
Es ist ein schleichend Grün,
das in ein Dunkel schleicht.
Das Dunkel ist die Nacht,
die bald in aller Welt
auf allem Schnee wird sein,
auf allem Grün wird sein.
Hin schleicht sich freundlich Grün
ins Dunkel, ach wie schön.
Am Fenster sehe ich's.

AT THE WINDOW (II)

I see at the window,
so nice,
outside, it's not much.
There's a little snow
on which it rains now.
There's a creeping green
that creeps into the darkness.
Darkness is night,
soon it will cover the world,
it will cover the snow,
it will cover the green.
This kind green creeping
into the darkness; oh how nice.
At the window I see it.

ALLES GRÜN

Die Wiesen ziehen leis
das sanfte Grün mit fort
und führen wieder her
das Grün, bald ist es nah
bald ist es wieder weit,
so weit, daß sich in mir
die Angst, die Sehnsucht regt.
Und Sehnsucht ist doch tot
und Bangen ist doch tot.
Die Wiesen ziehen leis
die tote Angst heraus
aus meinem Herzen, dann
wird wieder alles still.
Und alle Welt seh ich
mit schönen Wiesen voll.
Ich mag auch schaun, wohin,
mit grünen Wiesen voll
und nur mit Grün, mit Grün
das treulich stille hält,
ist voll die ganze Welt.

EVERYTHING GREEN

Gently the meadows draw out,
take up this calm green
and bring it back,
this green, soon it is near,
soon again it is far,
so far that my fear,
my longing stir inside me.
And a longing is dead
and a terror is dead.
Gently the meadows draw
the dead fear out
of my heart, then
everything is still again.
And I see all the world
filled by beautiful meadows.
Wherever I look, too,
filled by green meadows,
and only with green, with a green
that remains unfailingly still,
is the whole world full.

DAS GELIEBTE

Ich hebe die Gardine:
Ich sehe goldne Sonne
auf grünen Wiesen glänzen.
Ich sehe blauen Himmel
auf grünen Wiesen glänzen.
Ich sehe Sonn und Himmel
auf grüne Wiesen lachen.
Ich senke die Gardine
und seh mich um im Zimmer.
Das Zimmer ist voll Sonne.
Das Zimmer ist voll Himmel.
Wie schön ist das, Geliebte!
Ich spreche und ich lache:
mein Zimmer ist ein Himmel.
Ich liebe doch den Himmel.
Wie schön ist das, Geliebte!

THE BELOVED

I lift the curtain:
I see the golden sun
shining on green meadows.
I see the blue sky
shining on green meadows.
I see sun and sky
laughing on green meadows.
I lower the curtain
and look around the room.
The room is full of sun.
The room is full of sky.
How beautiful, my beloved!
I speak and I laugh:
my room is a sky.
How I love the sky.
How beautiful, my beloved!

UNTER GRAUEM HIMMEL

Unter grauem Himmel,
unter schwerem Himmel,
steht das weiße Häuschen.
In dem weißen Häuschen,
in dem kleinen Zimmer
sitze traurig ich.

Durch entlaubte Bäume,
durch vernäßte Bäume
sucht und sieht mein Auge,
findet arme Wiesen.
Wegen diesen Wiesen
wein' ich bitterlich.

UNDER A GRAY SKY

Under a gray sky,
under a heavy sky,
there's a small white house.
Inside the small white house,
in this little room,
I sit sad.

Through leafless trees,
through wet trees,
my eye searches and sees,
finds poor meadows.
On behalf of these meadows
I cry bitterly.

ABENDLIED

Es gehen noch wenige Leute umher,
ein einzelner noch, dann keiner mehr.

Es möchte sich legen auf Haus und Flur
so etwas wie Müdigkeit der Natur.

Es lächelt so fein um Baum und Baum.
Das Lächeln jedoch unterscheidet man kaum.

Was doch ein Windlein armselig ist,
das noch am Abend die Welt bemißt.

Mich kommt ein Zögern und Schlafen an;
ich betrachte nur noch den ernstesten Mann,

den Mond, der sehr an Bedeutung gewinnt,
sobald die Sonne der Welt entrinnt.

EVENING SONG

Only a few people are still walking about,
now there's one left, and then they're all gone.

Something like the weariness of nature
wants to lie down on the houses and fields.

Its subtle smile moves from tree to tree,
but you can barely recognize it.

How miserable is the small breeze
that still travels the evening world.

I begin to feel hesitant and tired;
I consider only the gravest man,

the Moon, who grows more important,
as soon as the sun breaks free from the earth.

BIERSZENE

Einer scherzte mit der Kellnerin.
Einer stützte müde seinen Kopf.
Einer spielte seelenvoll Klavier.
Einem brach das Lachen aus dem Mund.
Einem schoß das Dunkel durch den Traum.
Einem gab die harte Taste nach.
Einmal lief das schlanke Mädchen fort.
Einmal fuhr der blöde Träumer auf.
Einmal war das Spiel ein englisch Lied.

Ein verbuhlter Schwätzer, Tabakrauch,
ein erwachter Träumer, und ein Traum,
ein ermüdeter Klaviervirtuos.

BEER SCENE

One frolicked with the waitress.
One propped his tired head.
One played the piano full of soul.
One's laughter burst from his mouth.
One's dream was shot by darkness.
One's hard key gave in.
Once the slender girl ran away.
Once the stupid dreamer flared up.
Once the game was an English song.
A tricked gossiper, tobacco smoke,
a woken dreamer, and a dream,
a tired piano virtuoso.

From
FURTHER SELECTIONS
(1897-1905)

TRÜBER NACHBAR

Es liegt schon da wie ein anderes Haus,
doch dringt den ganzen Tag hinaus
das Schreien armer Kinder.
Die Kinder der «bessern» Leute sind
geschwind beim Ohrläppchen gefaßt, geschwind,
die der Armen noch zweimal geschwinder.
O daß zu Not und Mangel muß
auch noch Gehässigkeit setzen den Fuß,
und daß der Haß zuvor
sich alle Armen zum Opfer erkor.

Es liegt schon da wie ein anderes Haus,
doch dringt den ganzen Tag hinaus
das Weinen armer Kinder.

GLOOMY NEIGHBOR

It does sit there like another house,
but all day long the screaming
of poor children leaks out.
The children of "better" people
are seized promptly by the ears, promptly,
and the ones of the poor twice as fast.
Oh that spite must now add
its foot to misery and despair,
that all the poor have already
been chosen as hate's first victims.

It does sit there like another house,
but all day long the crying
of poor children leaks out.

FEIERABEND

Ich bin, nachdem ich den Tag
verbracht, im Fieber heimgegangen.
Auf dem ganzen Heimweg lag
die Sonne auf meinen Wangen.

Die seelige Abendglut
lag breit auf allen Wiesen
und ich nannte diesen
Schein mein verströmtes Blut.

Mein heißes brennendes Blut
lag tröstend über aller Welt.
So ging ich im Übermut –
Jetzt war ja alles bestellt.

Ich wußte nicht, wie mir geschah,
ich lehnte mich an einen Hag,
in mein Blut, das nah
und weit auf den Wiesen lag.

CLOSING TIME

After a spent day, I
walked back in a fever.
The whole way home
the sun touched my cheeks.

The blissful evening glow
spread across the meadows
and I called this light
the blood I shed.

My hot burning blood lay
consoling the entire world.
So I walked with pride—
Now that all was tilled.

I didn't know what was happening,
I leaned against a fence post,
in my blood that covered
the meadows near and far.

MUTLOS

Die stille Trauer
besuchte mich,
ich senkte mich
in ihre Schauer,

darin ich spürte
nicht Sorg' nicht Hast,
nur schwere Last.
Die Trauer führte

dann so mich weiter
durch dunklen Gram,
bis wieder kam
ans Licht der Schreiter.

Ich bat sie leise:
behalte mich –
sie aber wich
auf neue Reise.

FAINT-HEARTED

Silent grief
visited me,
I lowered myself
into its chill,

I felt there
not fear, not haste,
only a heavy burden.
Grief led me

further on
through a dark sorrow,
until this striding
returned to the light.

I bade softly:
keep me—
but it moved on
to a new journey.

TRAUERSPIEL

Der Vorhang geht hinauf zur ernsten Höhe:
Es zeigt das Spiel sich, und das Stück beginnt.
Die Männer machen stolze Kämpfermienen,
verzerren den Mund zu einem bösen Lächeln,
das Tod verspricht, schon eh die Wunde springt
und Blut die blassen Stirnen rosig färbt.
Ein Todentschloßner schlitzt den Bauch sich auf.
Sein Sohn schreit draußen vor der Tür, die Tür
bricht ein, und, wie zu Stein erstarrt, sieht er
das grausige Schauspiel an – er kam zu spät.
Die Szene wechselt, und das Auge sieht
in eines Gartens Traum hinein: Der Mann
stürzt riesenhaft vergrößert und entsetzlich
verändert aus den dunkeln Büschen vor,
langsam und schmeidig; und gespenstisch flattert
ein schwarzer Mantel um die Glieder ihm,
die weit ausholend tragische Schritte messen
auf dem Parkett der Bühne. Dann ein Kampf,
ein Ringen, daß die zornigen Knochen krachen.
Der eine stürzt, wie'n Vögelchen noch hüpfend,
bis er sich schrecklich überschlägt. Der andre
muß fliehn, doch bringt man ihn gefangen her
und kündet ihm des Urteils Willen an.
An allem ist ein kleines Mädchen schuld,
das kaum gelernt vernünftig hat zu lächeln.
So süß wie sündhaft, schuldlos wie gelehrt
in Künsten schon der Schuld, tritt sie voran
als helles Licht, Liebreiz und Schrecken werfend
in das Gemüt der bangen Hörerschaft.
Ihr trauernd nach lischt eine Fackel aus.

TRAGEDY

The curtain goes up to the grave height:
The play appears, and the piece begins.
The men with proud battle faces
twist their mouths into evil grins
that promise death, already wounds burst
open and blood stains pale brows rosy.
The one determined to die slits open his belly.
His son screams outside the door, the door
collapses, and, as if turned to stone, he watches
the gruesome sight—he was too late.
The next scene, and the eye peers
into a garden's dream: the man,
enlarged, colossal and terribly
deformed, plunges from the dark
bushes, slow and supple; and a black
cloak flaps like a specter around his limbs
reaching wide to measure the tragic steps
on the wooden stage. Then a fight,
a struggle that makes the mad bones crack.
One of them drops, trips like a little bird
until he tumbles horribly. The other
must flee, but they bring him back a prisoner
and announce the intended judgment.
The little girl is to blame for everything,
she who just barely learned to smile
with reason. Sweet like sin, innocent yet
already skilled in the art of guilt, she
steps forth as a bright light, tossing charm
and horror into the minds of the anxious audience.
Mourning after her, a torch goes out.

From
POEMS WRITTEN IN BIEL
(1919-1920)

FRÜHLING (I)

Es paßt wohl jedem, daß es wieder
warm ist, und daß die Fenster offen sind
und Frühlingswind ins Zimmer weht.
Vermutlich nimmt es niemand übel,
daß nun die Wälder wieder grünen
und Wiesen voller Gräser sind
und Vögel in den Bäumen singen
und Veilchen aus der Erde blühn.
Vielhunderttausend grüne Blätter!
Der Frühling ist ein Feldmarschall,
dem alle Leute gerne gönnen,
daß er die Welt bezwingt.
Siegreich durch alle Länder zieht sich
ein Blütenmeer. Die Gegenden
sind weiß, als wolle eine
Prinzessin angefahren kommen. O,
so zart ist alles, viel zu zart,
als daß es Dauer haben könnte.
Der Frühling ist nur kurz, was red' ich
für altgebacknes Zeug. Das weiß
ja jeder. Kinderspiel im Freien!
«Ist's möglich?» fragen sich die Menschen
und schaun sich an und lächeln. Einer
weint gar vor Freude. Schwierig ist's,
in all das Herrliche zu sehn
und nicht gerührt zu sein. Der Frühling

SPRING (I)

Surely everyone's happy that it's warm
again, and that the windows are open,
that a spring wind blows into the room.
Presumably no one minds
that the woods are greening again,
that meadows are full of grass,
that birds are singing in the trees,
that violets are blooming from the dirt.
Hundreds and thousands of green leaves!
Spring is a field marshal
who conquers the world,
and no one holds a grudge.
A victorious sea of blossoms
drifts across the lands. The regions
are white, as though a princess
were about to arrive. Oh,
everything's so delicate,
too delicate to last.
But what foolish talk; spring is
brief, everyone knows that.
A child's play in the open.
"Is it possible?" people wonder
and look at each other and smile. One
even cries with joy. It's difficult
to face all this glory and not be
moved. Though spring has been here

war oft schon da und ist doch jedes
mal neu und immer wieder jung.
Das Alte geht mit Jungem. Gatte
mit Gattin. Kleines mit dem Großen,
und alle sind verbrüdert: Völker
mit Völkern. Zur Geliebten schleicht
der Liebende. Er singt. Nur dem,
der wahrhaft liebt, gelingt ein Lied.
Küssen und Träumen. – Unweit steht
mit finstrer Mien' an einer Mauer
der Lebensernst; und wer an ihm
vorübergeht, muß zittern.

before, time and time again
it's new and always youthful.
The old walks with the young. Husband
with wife. The small with the great,
and all are made brothers: nations
with nations. The lover sneaks
to his beloved. He sings. Only he
who truly loves achieves a song.
Kissing and dreaming.—Nearby,
with a sinister face, life's gravity
is standing by a wall; and whoever
walks past it, must tremble.

OKTOBER

Die Blätter fallen von den Bäumen,
Das Grün verwandelt sich in Gelb,
und zarter Hauch umgibt das Land.
Oktober hat ein freundliches
Gesicht; gleicht er nicht einem feinen,
vornehmen Herrn, schenkt er dir nicht
Äpfel und Birnen und die saft'gen
Trauben und Nüsse? Zwar gibt's keine
so schönen, warmen Nächte mehr,
doch sind die Tage immer noch
blau, und an Wärme fehlt es nicht.
Oktober mahnt uns an den Dichter
Lenau und an ein Wandern. Prächtig
ist letztres nun; du gehst über
ein Feld und kommst dann in den Wald,
der hell und sonnig ist, daß es
dich glücklich macht, und still und lauter
und klar dir die Gedanken durch
die Seele gehen. Geht nicht etwas
Geistvolles, Seelenvolles jetzt
im friedlichen Bereich umher?
Im Herbst war ich von jeher ruhig,
glaubte an ihn, wie an etwas
Glückbringendes und schaut' mit ganz
besondrer Freude in den Himmel
und rund herum ins Leben, das mir

OCTOBER

Leaves are falling from the trees,
green changes into yellow,
and a delicate breeze circles the land.
October has a friendly face;
doesn't it resemble a genteel,
noble gentleman, doesn't it offer
you apples and pears and succulent
grapes and nuts? Although
the beautiful, warm nights
are gone, the days are still blue,
and there's no lack of warmth.
October reminds us of the poet
Lenau and walking. The latter
is now splendid; you walk across
a meadow and then enter the forest,
which is so bright and sunny,
it makes you happy, and quiet
and louder and clearer thoughts
pass through your soul.
Isn't something spirited, soulful
walking around in this peaceful realm?
I've always been calm in autumn,
believed in it, like a symbol of luck,
and looked up at the sky with extreme
joy and all around at life
that then seemed almost exalted.

alsdann beinah geadelt vorkam.

Die Blumen freilich müssen welken,
auch Menschen werden älter, nun, das
muß ja so sein, doch denke ich,
und du magst ähnliches dir denken,
daß es ein neues Blühen gibt,
und daß es auch ein früheres
Blühen gegeben hat, das mit dir
durch alles fernere Erleben
geht und nicht schwindet, weil es hinter
dir liegt. Die Liebe, die du fühltest,
und all das Gute und das Schöne,
das sich dir gab, dein Streben, dein
Errungenes, obwohl vielleicht nun
im schatt'gen Dämmer, schimmern dir
hell, und sind unverwelklich, drum
sei froh, sei sanft und gütig und
geduldig.

Flowers must indeed wither,
people too grow older,
that's how it should be,
yet I think, and you may be
thinking the same,
that there exists a new bloom,
and a former bloom, that follows
you through past experiences
and never dwindles, because it
lies behind you. Despite the love
you felt, and all the good
and beautiful that gave
itself to you, your striving,
your achievements that now,
fadeless, glisten brightly
in twilight's shadows,
be glad, be gentle and kind
and patient.

NACH ZEICHNUNGEN VON DAUMIER

Vor einem Spiegel steht ein Dichter,
später brilliert er im Salon
mit Rezitation von Versen.

In eine Stube guckt ein Landmann.
«Bonjour, Madame», sagt er, und lüftet
den Hut, das hübsche Frauchen lächelt.

Auf staub'ger Straße rollt ein Wagen,
vorn lenkt der Herr, und hinten sitzt
sein Diener. «Wohin geht die Fahrt?»
Möchten es gar zu gerne wissen.

Potztausend, wer liegt da im Gras?
Der fühlt sich offenbar hier wohl,
sonst wär' vielleicht er auch wo anders.
Auf alle Fälle scheint er uns
nicht sehr vom Geist der Zeit beeinflußt.

Wir sind in einem Kaffeehaus.
«Hell oder dunkel?» fragt der Kellner.
Der Gast erwidert: «Ganz wie's Ihnen
paßt». Ist das nicht ein droll'ger Kauz?

Einer sitzt im Vergnügungsboot,
da fährt ein Dampfer auf ihn zu,

AFTER DRAWINGS BY DAUMIER

A poet stands in front of a mirror,
later he shines in the salon
with his recitation of verses.

A peasant peeks into a living room.
"Bonjour, Madame," he says, and lifts
his hat, the pretty mistress smiles.

A car goes down a dusty road,
the master is at the wheel, and the servant
sits in the back. "Where are we going?"
They would love to know.

I'll be damned, who's that lying in the grass?
Seems like he's quite comfortable here,
otherwise he would probably be somewhere else.
In any case, it doesn't look like he's been
affected much by the spirit of the times.

We are in a coffeehouse.
"Pale or dark?" asks the waiter.
The customer replies, "As you see
fit." Isn't he an odd fellow?

A man sits in a pleasure boat, when
suddenly a steamer heads towards him,

er ruft: «O weh mir, je suis perdu».
Verloren glaubte sich schon mancher
und war's zum Glück dann doch noch nicht.

Das Beste kommt zuletzt: ein Herr
sitzt beim Friseur, da sieht er plötzlich
ein Liebespaar vorübergehn,
er rennt hinaus mit eingeseiftem
Gesicht, steht starr, als säh' er Geister,
und sagt: «Was seh' ich, c'est ma femme.»

he shouts: "Oh dear, je suis perdu."
Many have believed themselves lost
but luckily in the end they were not.

And the best for last: a gentleman sits
in a barbershop, when he suddenly
sees a pair of lovers go by,
he runs outside with a lathered
face, stands frozen, as if he's seen ghosts,
and says: "What's this, c'est ma femme."

From
POEMS WRITTEN IN BERNE
(1924-1933)

WIE DIE HÜGELCHEN LÄCHELTEN

Hättest du die Bäumchen
stehn gesehn, mir war's, als ob
sie tänzelten, so lustig
gestikulierten sie, ein Wölkchen
sah in silberweißer Reinlichkeit
einem Delphin ähnlich, hättest du
die vielen Hügelchen gelblich-grünlich
lächeln sehen können, schade,
daß du den Eisenbahnzug nicht sahest,
der nun auf golden-schwarzer Schiene
gewichtig und zart, leise und gewaltig,
schwerfällig-schön und mühsam
und doch in herrlicher Leichtigkeit vorbeifuhr.
Unendlich bedauerlich finde ich,
daß du nicht auch sehen konntest,
wie die Fahrgäste aus den Wagenfenstern blickten.
Einer wie der andere schaute auf mich,
der im Gras lag,
die Stufen eines Stegleins zählte,
das einen Abhang hinauflief,
die Brücken mit Blicken
inspizierte, und der an der Brust der Erde
glücklich war.
Ein Fabrikrohr
sich in die Höhe verlor,
ein Mädelchen in einiger Entfernung spazierte.

HOW THE SMALL HILLS SMILED

You should've seen
the little trees, their gestures
were so funny, it felt like
they were dancing, in its silver-
white cleanliness a small cloud
resembled a dolphin, you
should've seen the small hills
smiling yellow-green, it's a shame
you didn't see the train
that passed by on gold-black rails,
severe and gentle, quiet
and massive, beautifully sluggish
and laborious yet marvelously light.
And it's infinitely regrettable
you also couldn't see the passengers
staring out the windows.
One like the other stared at me,
who lay in the grass,
counting the timber steps
leading up the hillside,
who looked over the bridges,
and who was happy
in earth's bosom.
A factory chimney
lost itself into the heights,
a little girl walked in the distance.

Ich meinte, ich müsse,
alles rings in solchem Glück,
in solcher Heiterkeit zu sehn,
feengleich vergehn,
bog den Kopf zurück:
O, war das schön!
Ziele gibt es viele, zu sein an einem Ziel,
dazu braucht's nicht viel.

I thought, seeing everything around me
in such happiness, such cheerfulness,
I ought to dissolve fairylike
and bent my head backwards:
Oh, how beautiful that was!
There are so many ends,
But it doesn't take much
To be at one.

SONNTAGVORMITTÄGLICHE FAHNEN

In bleichem Schimmer blitzen
erschrockene Laternen.
In was für Fernen
fliegt ihr, Wolken, und wo sitzen
sonst noch im Sonnenschein Menschen auf Bänken?
Wie schön sich Fahnen,
als wollten sie mich an etwas mahnen,
vom Licht durchstrahlt und sich ringelnd,
wie Kinder, die singelnd
spielen und glücklich sind,
und wie Rosen, die von leisem Wind
leicht geschaukelt werden, zu den Bäumen,
die mich sonntagvormittäglich träumen
machen, niedersenken.

SUNDAY MORNING FLAGS

Startled lanterns flicker
in a pale glow.
Into what distances
are you flying, clouds, and where else
in this sunshine are people still sitting on benches?
How lovely the flags,
as if they wanted to remind me of something,
sunlit and winding,
like children playing,
singing and happy,
and like roses, swaying
in a gentle breeze, towards the trees,
which make me dream on a Sunday
morning, sink down.

EMPFINDUNG

Was mir so lange noch vor Augen lag,
was mich erheiterte, und was mich doch nicht
ruhig zu machen hat vermocht, Natur,
wird über kurzem weit, weit draußen sein.
Ich werde es entbehren und begeistert
besingen, dieses Leuchten, dieses Klingen
von Schällen und von Farben. Irgendwie
werd' ich's vermissen und drum doppelt lieben,
als wäre es ein Rätsel mir geblieben.
Üb'rall ist's schön,
sobald nur innerlich wir irgend etwas Schönes sehn.
Horche nicht falschem Flehn.
Was du bewahrst, wird immer mit dir gehn.

SENSATION

What was for so long before my eyes,
what made me cheer up, and yet what
could not calm me, nature,
will very soon be far, far outside.
I will do without it and with delight
sing the praise of its brilliance, this earsplitting
of sounds and colors. Somehow
I will miss it and so redouble my love,
as if it were still a riddle to me.
It's beautiful everywhere,
as long as we see beauty from within ourselves.
Don't listen to false insistence.
Something you enshrine will always be with you.

DIE JAHRESZEITEN

Wenn man beliebt bei sich will sein,
stellt man sich allerlei Ergötzlichkeiten vor,
zum Beispiel, daß der Frühling wunderschön sei
wie ein aus seinem Bettchen lächelndes
Kind, und der Sommer, bildet man sich ein,
sei eine junge, kapriziöse Frau; Herbst ist
ein talentierter Knabe, mit den Trauben
erstmaligen Vergeistigtseins geschmückt,
und Gassen eines mittelalterlichen
Städtchens und Wimpel eines Segelschiffes,
umzaubert von der kühlen Atmosphäre.
Frag' ich mich, was der Winter wäre,
so freu' ich mich, eh' ich ihn mir erkläre,
ein halbes Stündchen lang an seinem frischen
Antlitz; mit einem Mädchen komme ich sodann
her und behaupte, daß des Winters heil'ges
Einsamsein jungfrauhaft mich dünkt.
Die Jahreszeiten gleiten wie im Kreise
um mein inwendiges und äußres Sein.
Im Frühling zwitschern Vögelein
bald laut, bald leise.
Vom Kind an, das mit Reifen spielt, geht es
treppaufwärts bis zur goldigen
Höhe der Lebenskraft und neigt sich
auf einem Stab beim Greise.

THE SEASONS

When one wants to be popular with one's self,
one imagines all kinds of delights,
that spring is wonderful like a child
smiling from her little bed, for example,
and summer, one fancies,
is a young, capricious woman; autumn is
a talented boy, adorned with the grapes
of the first spiritualization,
and alleyways of a medieval town
and streamers on a sailboat,
enchanted by the cool atmosphere.
When I ask myself, what would winter be,
I'm delighted for half an hour, before
I explain him to myself, by his fresh
face; thereafter I arrive with a girl
and claim that winter's holy
solitude seems virginal to me.
The seasons move almost in a circle
around my internal and external being.
In spring birds twitter,
sometimes loudly, sometimes softly.
Past the child who plays with hoops,
it goes up the steps to the golden
height of the will to live and down
to settle on the old man's staff.

WIE ICH EIN BLATT FALLEN SAH

Hätte ich mich nicht nach
den zum Teil bereits nackten
Zweigen umgedreht, so würde mir
der Anblick des langsam-
goldig zu Boden fallenden,
aus üppigem
Sommer stammenden Blattes
entgangen sein. Ich hätte etwas
Schönes nicht gesehen und etwas Liebes,
Beruhigendes und Entzückendes,
Seelenfestigendes nicht empfunden. Schaue öfter
zurück, wenn es dir
dran liegt, dich zu bewahren.
Mit Gradausschauen ist's nicht getan.
Die sahen nicht alles, die nicht rund um sich sah'n.

HOW I SAW A LEAF FALLING

Had I not turned
around for the already
partly naked branches,
I would've missed
the sight of a lush
summer's leaf falling
slow and golden.
I would not have seen
something beautiful and felt
something lovely, calm
and charming, soul-hardening.
Look back more often,
if you want to save yourself.
Nothing is done by looking straight ahead.
Those who never looked around, didn't see it all.

FESTZUG

Defekte Elemente machten sich
auch diesmal selbstverständlich wieder geltend;
ich denke an ein wicht'ges Sichgebärden,
übrigens reim' ich dies Gedicht hier nicht,
damit es nicht als spielerisch empfunden
wird, und weil ich das Dichten heute mir
zum Kinderspiele machen will, o, einen,
der eine rosige Verlagsanstalt
im Grünen gründete, wobei er pleite
ging, sah ich in der Menschenmenge stehen.
Ein Zug von Kostümierten schritt vorüber.
Ein'ge kamen zum Schauspiel spät und andre
standen schon da, eh's was zu sehen gab;
am schönsten schien mir eine Amazone
zu sein, die auf dem Pferd saß, wie wenn Scharen
von Gläubigen am einsamschönen Ziel
sehnsücht'gen Wanderns angekommen seien.
Verständlich wird man finden, daß ich sage,
ein Ungeheuer hätt' mich int'ressiert
um zähneweisender Berachung willen.
Gespielt war alles nur, und die Dämonen
hatten im Sinn, sich einen Doppelliter
später an heimeligem Ort zu leisten.
Ein Mädchen in der Tracht der Ländlerin
gab vor, sie weine; herrlich sah ein Wagen,
der eine Hochzeit zu vergegenwärt'gen

PARADE

Flawed elements naturally
asserted themselves again this time;
I'm thinking of important behavior,
incidentally, I'm not going to use rhyme
in this poem, so as not to make it sound
playful, and because today I want to turn
poetry into a children's game, oh, I saw
the founder of a publishing house
coming up rosy amid the countryside
that ruined him standing in the crowd.
A line of costumed people passed by.
Some arrived late for the show, others stood
there already before there was anything to see;
to me the Amazon seemed the most beautiful,
sitting on her horse, as if hoards of believers
had, after a journey of longing, arrived
at a beautiful and secret destination.
One will understand when I say
that I might've found a monster interesting
for the sake of its fang-pointed advice.
But it was all play, and the demons
were already thinking about their
large beers later at the cozy place.
A girl dressed as a peasant
pretended to cry; beautiful seemed
the wagon that brought to mind

schien, aus, und schwebend gleitete ein Haus
vorbei, das sich die Bauenden mit Liedern,
die zickzackförmig in den Himmel stiegen,
zusammenzimmerten. Die Köchin drohte
zierlich mit ihrer Kelle, und ein Schreiber
aus farbenfröhlichem Jahrhundert strotzte
von tintenfässeligem Gleichgewicht.
Ein Fahnenschwinger ließ die Landesfahne
wie einen Tänzer in die Höhe klimmen;
sie fiel ihm immer wieder wie ein Eigen-
tum in die Hand; mir scheint, daß allem Können
man billig ein'gen Beifall dürfe gönnen.

a wedding, and a house, knocked
together by the builders' songs
zigzagging to heaven, floated by.
The female cook threatened gracefully
with her ladle, and out of colorful
centuries a scribe was radiant
with the poise of an inkwell.

A flag thrower who like a dancer
let the country flag climb into the air;
it fell always, like a possession,
back into his hand; it seems every skill
deserves a quick applause.

DAS SEHNEN

Das Fleisch, das Bier, das Brot,
das man verbraucht an allen Tagen,
wie soll ich dies nur hurtig sagen?
Du immer mich durchziehndes Sehnen,
wie Flüsse rauschen, Ebenen sich dehnen,
so mutet es mich an, und Frauen
gibt es, die mir zu schreiben sich getrauen,
sie seien mir einmal an einem lauen
Abende gut gewesen, ihre Briefe
atmen gemessne Kühle aus und Tiefe
des Denkens und Empfindens, sie vergaßen –
und, wie sie nun vielleicht am Nähtisch saßen,
erinnerten sie sich nach vielen Jahren,
wie sie bewegt von irgend etwas waren,
spielen gedankenvoll mit ihren Haaren.
Mein Sehnen, und das Sehnen aller andern
bunt durcheinander wandern.

LONGING

The meat, the beer, the bread
one consumes every day,
how shall I say this quickly?
You, my ever-pervading longing,
like the rush of rivers, the widening of plains,
that's how it appears to me, and women
exist who dare to write
how they were once good to me
for a pleasant evening, their letters
breathe a measured coolness and a depth
of thought and feeling they've forgotten—
and, perhaps now sitting at a sewing table,
remembering after many years
how they were moved by something,
they play thoughtfully with their hair.
My longing, and the longing of everyone else
drift, tangle in the muss.

HERBST (II)

Man denkt im Herbst an Künstler und an Dichter,
die ihre Existenz dem Schönen weihn.
Das gelbe Laub, das an den Bäumen prangt,
erinnert an ein tapeziertes Zimmer,
worin die Gnäd'ge mit dem Pagen schäkert.
Die goldnen Augen sind berückend schön,
die dieser kurzen Jahrszeit eigen sind,
die wie das Liebesglück des Liebenden
und wie die Illusion des Mädchens aussieht.
Warum wird man im Herbste träum'risch? Weil es
in allen, die im Leben tätig sind
und sich an seinen Äpfeln, Trauben freuen,
ein unaussprechliches Bedürfnis gibt,
von den Begehrlichkeiten auszuruhen?
O, durch wie viele Fehler geht der Mensch,
und liebt er grad aus diesem Grund des Herbstes
Gesicht mit dem verständnisvollen Lächeln?

AUTUMN (II)

In autumn we think of artists and poets
who dedicate their existence to the beautiful.
The trees ablaze with yellow leaves
resemble a wallpapered chamber
wherein a lady flirts with her bellboy.
This short season's inherent
golden eyes are enchanting,
like a lover's bliss
or the illusion of a girl.
Why are we so full of dreams in autumn?
Because there's an ineffable need
in whomever is part of life
and delights in apples and grapes
to give rest to all that greed?
Oh, how many mistakes does man commit,
and isn't this exactly the reason why he loves
autumn's face with its knowing smile?

DER LESER

Mit einem Bahnhofhallenbüchelein
setzt' er sich in ein Nest hinein.
Er sah von Hotelgouvernanten
sich angekränkelt, die ihn bannten.

Das Nest, wovon soeben ich gesprochen,
hat ihn mit seiner Heimlichkeit bestochen,
ein Plätzchen war's, von feinen Zweigen
beschattet, Amoretten neigen
sich dort ob ihm und seinem Lesen, Träumen,
um kosend ihm den Kopf zu säumen,
im Blätterreiche summen Fliegen,
die um den würz'gen Duft sich biegen,
und der, der in dem Büchlein liest,
glücklich ob dessen int'ressantem Inhalt ist,
güt'ge Blumen umschmeicheln ihn,
kostbare Zeit geht sorglos hin.

THE READER

With one of those train station dime store books,
he settled into his nest.
He saw how the hotel governesses banished
him with their disapproving stares.
The nest I've just mentioned
bribed him with its privacy,
it was a fine spot shaded
by delicate twigs, above him
and his book, his dreaming, the putti
dip down to his head with caresses,
flies are buzzing amid lush leaves
and turn towards the fragrant scent,
and he who is reading the little book,
happy with its interesting content,
surrounded by flowers soft and kind,
wastes precious time without a care.

LEBENSFREUDE

Wie schön ist's, wenn man ruhig ist
und zu sich selber nichts mehr sagt.
Da sieht man glückliche und schöne Menschen,
reizvoll zu einem Kreis vereinigt,
sich unter Bäumen an Gesprächen amüsieren,
niedliche Tänzerinnen sich im Takte
eines Konzerts bewegen. Die Natur
hat eine zuckerbäckerhafte Süßigkeit;
Kostüm', anmutige Gebärden! Auf dem Wasser
ergötzen solche, die in Booten schaukeln,
sich an dem Gleiten über einen Spiegel,
die Landschaft sieht gemäldeartig aus,
das Leben, bildet man sich ein, sei ewig,
unmöglich sei unangenehmes Scheiden
von blümeliggeschmückten, holden Weiden.
Wie ist das Sterben und sein herbes Leiden
schwer in ergieb'ge Worte einzukleiden.

JOY OF LIFE

How beautiful it is when you're silent,
when you stop talking to yourself.
There you see happy and beautiful
people, charmingly joined into a circle,
enjoying their conversations beneath
the trees, cute dancers who move
to the rhythm of a concert. Nature
is a sugar baker's confection; costumes,
elegant gestures! On the water
those who rock in boats delight
in their gliding over a mirror,
the landscape seems painted,
life, you imagine, is eternal,
and an unpleasant parting from these
gracious, flowered pastures, impossible.
How difficult it is to dress death
and his harsh suffering in fertile words.

SOMMER

Im Sommer ißt man grüne Bohnen,
Pfirsiche, Kirschen und Melonen.
In jeder Hinsicht schön und lang,
bilden die Tage einen Klang.

Durch Länder fahren Eisenbahnen,
auf Häusern flattern lust'ge Fahnen.
Wie ist's in einem Boote schön,
umgeben von gelinden Höhn.

Das Hochgebirge trägt noch Schnee,
die Blumen duften. Auf dem See
kann man mit Glücklichsein und Singen
vergnügt die lange Zeit verbringen.

Reich bin ich durch ich weiß nicht was,
man liest ein Buch und liegt im Gras
und hört von üb'rall her die dummen
unnützen Mücken, Fliegen summen.

SUMMER

In summer we eat green beans,
peaches, cherries and melons.
In every sense nice and long
the days form a sound.

Trains travel through the country,
flags flap merrily on rooftops.
How nice it is in a boat
surrounded by gradual heights.

The high peaks still wear snow,
flowers give fragrance. On the lake
you can spend all your time
singing and being happy.

I don't know what it is that makes me rich,
you lie in the grass and read a book
and from everywhere you hear
the pointless gnats, buzzing flies.

ANNEHMLICHKEIT DES KLAGENS

Niemand braucht sich verlassen vorzukommen,
doch denke ich, es gebe viele, die sich
einbilden, daß sie einsam sind.
Hier leb' ich wie ein Kind, bezaubert
von der Idee, daß ich vergessen worden bin.
Vielleicht gibt es nur wen'ge, die sich derart
erquicken können. Üb'rall sei ein wenig
Sonne, sage ich mir, und Wind und Schatten
und glänz'ge Freudenaugenblicke
und Trauer, adlerhaft aus Höhen .
des Menschseins auf die Seele niederstürzend.
Gewiß vergessen sich die Menschen schnell,
doch muß sich jeder meiner Meinung nach
schuld an dem Umstand geben,
daß die, die man vergessen hat, selbst wieder
vergeßlich ihrerseits gewesen sind.
Über etwas Natürliches zu klagen,
ist manchmal immerhin ganz angenehm.

THE COMFORT OF COMPLAINING

No one should feel abandoned,
yet I think there are many
who imagine themselves to be alone.
Here I live like a child, enchanted
by the idea that I've been forgotten.
Perhaps there are only a few of us who can
bounce back in this way. There's a bit of sun
everywhere, I say, and wind and shadows
and sparkling moments of happiness
and sorrow, swooping down on the soul
like an eagle from the heights of humanity.
Of course, people forget each other quickly,
but I believe everyone's
to blame for the fact
that those who were forgotten
were forgetful themselves.
To complain about something so natural
has a certain comfort sometimes.

SCHLAF

Wie unbedeutend doch das Leben ist,
es mutet wie ein freundliches Gesicht an,
worin man nicht viel Int'ressantes sieht.
Irgendwo wird Musik in einem Garten
gemacht, es wird spaziert, man ißt und trinkt
und geht und schläft, und an die Restaurants,
und an die tägliche und sonst'ge Arbeit
haben sich alle, die sich sagen, daß sie
Mitglieder der Gesellschaft sind, gewöhnt.
Das, was man als Bewegung und so weiter
empfindet, ähnelt einem Schlaf. Vergessen
einander nach und nach so gut wie alle
in weiten Lebens seltsam-heller Halle?

SLEEP

But how insignificant is life,
it seems like a friendly face
without much that's interesting.
Music is being played somewhere
in a garden, we take a stroll, eat
and drink and walk and sleep,
and everyone who claims to be
a member of society is used to
restaurants, jobs and other business.
That which we see as movement
and so on resembles sleep. Do we
all forget each other, one after another,
in life's strange bright hall?

DAS SCHÖNE

Da dachten alle nur noch an den Magen,
ich meine, an die Köstlichkeit der Küche,
an die Vollkommenheit der äußeren
Erscheinung, daran, daß sie den und den
untadelhaften Eindruck machen würden,
Kleidung und Wohnung und das freud'ge Lächeln,
aber in immer größere Entfernung
gingen die Herzen; Mut zu haben war verpönt,
sie waren sicher alle sehr verwöhnt,
weil sie sich so vernünftig, ungemein
richtig Notwendiges zu fassen wußten,
doch nach dem Fühlen sehnten sie sich sehr,
das Fühlen war schon längst nicht Mode mehr,
wo flöge dieses Schöne für sie her?

THE BEAUTIFUL

And everyone's just thinking about their stomachs,
I mean, of dishes prepared in the kitchen,
of the perfection of outward
appearances, of such and such
impeccable impression they would make,
clothes and house and happy smiles,
but the hearts moved farther
and farther away; courage was frowned upon,
they were all very satisfied with themselves,
because they acted so reasonably, knew
how to properly deal with what's necessary,
yet they very much yearned for emotions,
emotions were no longer fashionable,
and where would something beautiful come from?

HOHE SCHULE

Beim Warten, beim Enttäuschtsichfühlen
wird keiner fehlen.
So vorteilhaft er sich auch mag vermählen,
wird er sich selber unterwühlen.
Auf den Theaterstühlen
sitzt man am liebsten nun mit kühlen,
vornehmen, feinen, klugen Abneigungen,
und wenn das Stück hat ausgeklungen,
zieht man mit schicklicher Verdrossenheit
nach Hause. Keiner ist gescheit,
der nicht, wie Verdi, noch mit achtzig Jahren
mit einem Werk kam angefahren.
Alle in unsern Zeiten haben Schulden,
und keiner kommt daher zu kurz beim Dulden.

HIGH ART

No one will fail to attend
the waiting, the disappointment.
No matter how conveniently he marries,
he will dig himself into a hole.
The best way to sit on the chairs
of the theatre is with a cool,
elegant, delicate, intelligent aversion,
and when the show is over,
one returns home with a decent
frustration. No one is smart,
unless, like Verdi, they come
along at eighty with a new piece.
Nowadays everyone has debts,
and no one misses out on tolerance.

DAS SONETT VOM ZUCHTHAUS

Hier, wo die edelabgewogne Geste
galt, und wo wohlgeformte Redensarten
Anfragende gehorsam hießen warten,
wo beim gediegenen und prächt'gen Feste

manch Herz wohl zittert' unter seidner Weste
und Herrn und Damen in gewähltem, zarten
Betragen sich ergingen durch den Garten,
des Landes rings bedeutendste und beste

Gesellschaft unter zierlichen Allüren
auftrat, und wo die Klinken an den Türen
achtunggebietend glänzten, und Karossen

vierspännig an dem Volk vorüberschossen,
hier sehn sich heute solche eingeschlossen,
die so sind, daß man sie nicht soll berühren.

THE JAIL SONNET

Here, where nobly balanced gestures
held true, and where clean phrases
called on obediently waiting guests,
where many hearts trembled beneath silken vests

during dignified and splendid parties,
and ladies and gentlemen deported themselves
discreetly, tactfully through the garden,
the land's most eminent and finest

high society appeared and put on
airs, and where the imposing door
handles sparkled, and four-in-hands

raced past the common people,
here where those who shall not be touched
now find themselves locked up.

RÄTSEL

Wie kommt dem Lehrer strafbar vor ein liederlicher Schwänzer.
Sahst du schon je, daß Bäume tanzen wie gebundne Tänzer?

Ihre Bewegungslosigkeit ist zaub'rische Bewegtheit.
Häuser sind eine geh'nde, seh'nde, spring'nde Hingelegtheit.

Ähnlich ist's mit der Schönheitswirkung von verlaßnen Frauen,
schaffender Trägheit, mißtrauenumzittertem Vertrauen.

Ruinen können leben, Aufgerichtetes kann tot sein,
E. T. A. Hoffmann meint, zur Mozartoper passe Rotwein.

Du dich auf angenehmste Weise geistig, seelisch weitest,
wenn Fröhlichkeiten andrer du mit eigenen begleitest.

Sobald er dich zu seinem Mutwill'n fröhl'che Mien' sieht machen,
hört auch der ausgelassenste Verlacher auf mit Lachen.

Die Spötter sind am Ende doch nur Sehnende wie du,
und jedem schloß die Lebenstür sich irgendeinmal zu.

RIDDLES

How guilty a raffish slacker seems to the teacher.
Have you ever seen how trees move, dancers tied to the stake?

Their immobility is an enchanted motion.
The set-down houses that walk, see, leap.

It's like the beauty of jilted women,
the effect of productive indolence, faith's trembling mistrust.

Ruins can live, things erected can be dead,
E. T. A. Hoffmann believes a Mozart opera goes well with red wine.

It's quite easy to grow spiritually and intellectually
when your joy goes along with the joys of others.

As soon as he sees your willfully happy face,
even the most lighthearted laugher will quit his laughter.

In the end, the disdainful desire the same as you,
and life's door will inevitably have slammed on them.

DIE DAME IM REITKLEID

Aus den Wäldern ihrer Zerwühltheiten
steigt sie kühl
an den Tag des Nichtsbedürfens,
klingelt ihrem Diener,
daß er ihr die Schokolade bringe
und ihr von Selbstbesiegung singe
und liebt und haßt sich nicht
und schreibt dann ihrer schönen
Freundin, der Herrin von Langenthal,
einen von Besinnungen umzitterten,
kurzen, klugen, lieben
Brief, worin sie sich unschuldig und zugleich
erstaunlich weltgewandt gibt.
Nach beendigter Korrespondenz
parfümiert sie sich
und kommt sich reinlicher,
williger, verzichtender, aber auch
liebender vor, als je.
«Wie bin ich süß», sagt sie in einem Anflug
von vielleicht etwas leichtsinniger
Selbstwürdigung zu sich, die Reitpeitsche
überreicht ihr dann ihr Robert,
und nun reitet sie durch zweihundertjährige Alleen,
spendet mit ihrer Erscheinung Ermunterung,
indem sie Achtung erweckt.
Ob man sich achte, oder nicht, und ob man
uns glaube, oder nicht, hängt vom Talent ab.

LADY IN RIDING HABIT

From her rumpled woods
she rises coolly
into a day of no demands,
rings for her servant
to bring her chocolate
and to sing to her of self-defeat
and doesn't love or hate herself
and then writes a letter to her
beautiful friend, the Lady of Langenthal,
a letter girdled with reflections,
brief, clever, and sweet,
in which she pretends to be
at once innocent and amazingly worldly.
Finished with her correspondence,
she perfumes herself
and feels purer,
more eager, more sacrificing,
but also more loving than ever before.
"How sweet I am," she says,
with a sudden sense of careless
self-admiration, her Robert
hands her the riding whip,
and now she rides through two-hundred-year-old avenues,
her appearance attracts attention
and offers encouragement.
Whether or not they pay attention, and whether
or not they believe us, depends on talent.

DAS MÄDCHEN MIT DEN SCHÖNEN AUGEN

Die Bahnhofhalle wird mit weißer Farbe angestrichen,
ich sitze, wesentlich mit meinem Innern ausgeglichen,
im Menschentrubel, einer weiblichen Persönlichkeit,
die mich bald mustert und bald wieder ungemein gescheit
nicht auf mich achtet, in die Augen schauend. Wundervolle
Abwesenheiten, Gegenwärtigkeiten sind der Rolle
eigen, die sie nicht spielen will und dennoch, und wie gerne,
spielt, ihre Seele sagt ihr's, wie mir ihre Augensterne
lieb sind, und wie's mich zieht, bei ihr mein einzig echtes Leben
zu leben, doch sie weiß auch, wie ich bildendem Bestreben
gehorche, und so deckt sie denn, o, sähet ihr's, ihr Herr'n,
Höherm zu Ehr'n oftmals die Pracht, der ich mich nicht kann
wehr'n.

THE GIRL WITH THE BEAUTIFUL EYES

The station hall is getting painted white, I'm sitting,
considerably even keel with myself, crowds roiling
around me, looking at the eyes of a feminine personality,
who soon sizes me up and soon, ever so sensibly,
drops me from her view. There are wonderful absences,
presences inherent in this role she refuses to play,
but she plays it all the same, with pleasure, her soul tells her,
how much I love her two shinning stars, and how much
I'm drawn to her, how much I want to spend my one true life
with her, yet she also knows of my efforts to learn and create,
and so she often covers, oh, gentlemen, do you see it,
in honor of greatness, that splendor I'm unable to resist.

AN GEORG TRAKL

In irgendeinem fremden Lande würde ich
dich lesen, oder auch zu Hause,
und immer würden deine Verse mir zum Schmause
gereichen, und in einem ganz
bestimmten Sinne käme mich im Zimmer,
umglänzt vom Glanz und von dem Schimmer
der wundervollen Worte, die du fandest,
kein einz'ger trauriger Gedanke an.
Wie mit umschmeichelndem Gewande angetan,
erschiene ich mir in der Schlucht des Lesens,
in der Beschäft'gung mit der Schönheit deines Wesens,
das Schwan und Kahn und Garten und der Duft,
der draushinaufsteigt, ist, du blätterreiche,
unsäglich seelenvolle, weiche Eiche,
herabgefallner Felsblock, Schwänzeln
eines Mäuschens, eines Töchterchens Tänzeln,
verzagter Riese, hier auf einer Jurawiese
richte ich, spielerisch, als wenn ich träumte, diese
Ansprach' an deinen Genius.
Haben dich Hölderlin'sche Schicksalsfortsetzungen
in deiner Wiege und auf deiner Lebensbahn
umklungen und zu goldnem Wahn
bestimmt? Wenn ich Gedichte von dir lese,
ist mir, als trüg' mich eine präct'ge Chaise.

TO GEORG TRAKL

In some foreign land I would
read you, or even at home,
and always your verses would be
a feast, and in a very
specific sense in my room,
luminous and gleamy
with the wonderful words you found,
not a single sad thought would appear.
As if dressed in a fawning robe,
I found myself in the chasm of reading,
in the pursuit of your being's beauty
that is swan and boat and garden and the scent
that rises from it, you, soft, leafy,
ineffably soulful oak,
fallen boulder, the whipping tail
of a mouse, a young daughter's little jig,
rueful giant, here on a meadow in Jura
I dedicate this speech, playfully, dreamlike,
to your genius.
Have Hölderlin's perpetual Fates
in your cradle and on life's path
sung to you and marked your golden
madness? When I read your poems, I feel as if
I'm being driven away by a magnificent chaise.

DER GEFÄHRTE

Du wußtest ganz genau, daß ich und niemand
anders es war, dem du ge'nübersaßest,
ein-, zwei- und mehrmals, du erkanntest mich
und labtest dich an meinem Dichnichtkennen,
an der Unwissenheit, die dich für einen
Belieb'gen hielt, einen Hereingeschneiten,
für irgendwelchen zarten fils de famille.
Die Kaffeestube war gespickt von Gästen,
du durftest ungestört dich an mir weiden,
beispielsweis daran, daß ich sehr wahrscheinlich
mich linkisch, komisch, ungeschickt benahm,
oder daran, daß ich mich übermäßig
des Daseins freute, was geschehen kann,
wenn einer Zeitgenossen, die ihn prüfen,
nicht in der Näh' vermutet. Wir sind alle
nicht so, daß von der Luft wir leben können.
Herrlich wär's, wenn der Atem uns ernährte,
Erfolges Dauer unerschöpflich währte.
Irgendwie, ob du bist, was ich womöglich
nicht bin, bin ich auf Wiesen, Wegen und
in Häusern, unter Bäumen dein Gefährte,
den sich dein Denkvermögen nicht erklärte.

THE COMPANION

You knew exactly it was me and no one
else you sat across from,
once, twice, several times you recognized me
and delighted in my not-knowing-you,
in the ignorance that saw you as just
anyone, someone who arrived out of the blue,
any tender fils de famille.
The café was full of people,
undisturbed, you were allowed to feast your eyes
on me, on my likely clumsy, odd,
boorish manner, for instance,
or on my undue happiness to be
alive, which happens,
when one doesn't expect any fellows
nearby who study him. None of us
can live on air alone.
How splendid if breath could nourish us,
if success were inexhaustible.
Somehow, if you are what I'm possibly
not, on meadows, paths and in houses,
under trees, I'm your companion
inexplicable to your power of reason.

SELBSTSCHAU

Weil man nicht haben wollte, daß ich jung sei, wurd' ich jung.
Weil Leidender ich sollte sein, umschmeichelten mich viele Freuden.
Weil man in schlechte Laune mich zu setzen sich die größte Mühe gab,
suchte und fand ich Weg' in solche, wie ich sie willkommner mir nicht
wünschte.
Da man mir Ängstlichkeit einprägt', umjubelt' und umlachte mich der
Mut.
Dadurch, daß man im Stich mich ließ, lernte ich Selbstvergessen,
wodurch ich in die Lage kam, mich in Beseeltheiten zu baden.
Verlor ich viel, so sah und fühlt' ich, daß Verluste ein Gewinn sind,
da niemand etwas wiederfinden kann, wenn er es nicht vorher verlor,
und wiedersehen, was verloren ging, ist höherer Besitz als ständ'ger.
Indem man mich nicht kennen wollt', geriet ich auf die Kenntnis meiner
selbst,
wurde verständnisvoller, liebenswürd'ger Arzt an mir.
Weil ich im Leben Gegner fand, zog ich auch Freunde zu mir hin,
und Freunde fielen ab, doch Feind' auch hörten auf, feindlich zu sein,
und Unglück heißt der Baum, woran die schönsten Glückesfrüchte
wachsen.
Jeder trägt seine Lebensbahn in allem mit sich, was an Eigenheiten
Geburt, Umständ' zu Hause und die Schule ihm gegeben haben,
und Rettung braucht bloß der, dem's nicht gelang, sich nicht zu
überheben.
Niemals hatte ein mit sich Einverstandner Hilfe nötig,
falls ihm kein Unfall zustieß, daß man ins Spital ihn tragen mußte.

SELF-REFLECTION

Because they didn't want me to be young, I became young.
Because I should've been a sufferer, many pleasures flattered me.
Because they tried their best to put me in a bad mood,
I sought and found ways into moods more welcome than any I ever
                                                 could've wished for.
Since they impressed fear on me, courage cheered and laughed with
                                                 me.
They abandoned me, so I learned to forget myself,
which allowed me to bathe in my inspired soul.
When I lost much, I realized losses are winnings,
because no one can find something he didn't first lose,
and to discover what's lost is worth more than any safe possession.
Because they didn't want to know me, I became self-aware,
became my own understanding, friendly doctor.
Because I found enemies in my life, I attracted friends,
and friends dropped away, but enemies, too, stopped being hostile,
and the tree that bears the most beautiful fruits of luck is called
                                                 misfortune.
On life's path, we lift all the peculiarities given to us
by our birth, our family home and our schools,
and only those who couldn't help but strain themselves need to be
                                                 rescued.
No one who's content with himself ever needed help,
unless he happened to be in an accident and needed to be carried to the
                                                 hospital.

DER ARCHIVAR

Es kam einmal ein Archivar zu dem
Entschlusse, sich zu sagen, er sei müde,
und weil ihn das Bewußtsein nun durchdrang,
daß er den Lebensmut verloren habe,
sprach er zu sich: «Ich unglücksel'ger Knabe,
ich wanke.» Und das tat er in der Tat.
Von einer Ohnmacht wurde er ergriffen,
die Beine zitterten, die Last des Körpers
erschien ihm unerträglich schwer. Im Walde
sangen die sommerlichen Vogelkehlen;
das Jubilieren klang, als sei es glühend rot.
Ihm schien die Festigkeit komplett zu fehlen,
die Seel' ihm nicht den kleinsten Halt mehr bot,
er lächelte ironisch und war tot.

THE ARCHIVIST

There was once an archivist who
decided to tell himself he was tired,
and aware of the overwhelming fact
that he had lost his will to live,
he spoke to himself: "What a wretched lad,
I'm stumbling." And that's indeed what happened.
He was struck by a dead faint,
his legs were shaking, the weight of his body
seemed unbearable. In the forest
the birds of summer were singing;
their jubilation sounded glowing red.
His strength seemingly gone completely,
his soul unable to offer the slightest support,
he smiled wryly and died.

GLOSSE

Anläßlich eines Galaabends sprach ein nachmals großes Tier voll Huld zu
mir:
«Für mich steht außer Zweifel, daß Sie auserkoren sind zu nichts als zu
Plaisir.»

Wenn mich in Zukunft auch mit völligster Berecht'gung jemand
abkapiteln will,
dem sag' ich: «I'm Int'resse der Verständigung der Völker halte bitte dich
hübsch still.»

Wer einer Schul' entsprang, die von Napoleon gegründet worden ist, wie
ich,
für den ist's undenkbar, es könnte leicht ihm arrivier'n, er wär' uneins mit
sich.

Oft kann man Prachtgebäude abgespiegelt sehen in der ersten, besten
unscheinbaren Pfütze.
Wie zog ich einst vor einer leider längst inzwischen Hingesunknen
ehrerbietig meine Mütze.

Das Eintrittsgeld zu einem Dichtervortrag zahlt man vornehm an der
Kasse.
Beim Orgelspieler ich die Münze gnädig in die Kopfbedeckung fallen
lasse.

*

GLOSS

During a gala evening, full of grace a future big shot said to me:
"The way I see it, without a doubt, you're predestined to nothing other
than a life of pleasure."

If in the future someone wants to, even if fully justified, give me a
dressing down,
I'll tell him: "In the interest of the bond among races, why don't you just
be quiet."

For any graduate of a school founded by Napoleon, like me,
the thought of being at odds with oneself would be unimaginable.

Often one can see the reflection of a noble edifice in the first plain
puddle.
How I once tipped my hat in honor of one unfortunately long since dried
up.

One pays the admission fee for a poetry reading politely at the ticket
office.
With the street organist I kindly drop the coin into his hat.

One evening, in a good mood, I stood in front of an ironing shop,
waiting to pick up my
dress shirts, I remembered that it once housed the minister's office.

Ein's Abends stand ich stimmungsvoll vor einer Herrenkragenglätterei, die mich ersuchte, zu bedenken, daß sie einstmals Staatskanzlei gewesen sei.

Wenn mitten du im Wesentlichen bist, wo kannst du dann noch hin? Hauptsach' entgeht mir nicht, indessen ich ein bißchen nebensächlich bin.

When you're in the midst of the essential, where else can you go?
I don't miss out on the basics, even when I'm being a bit trivial.

DER GLÜCKLICHE

Menschen sind mund- und aug'- und ohrbegabt,
und Häuser haben Türe, Gänge, Fenster,
und in den Gassen, in den Sälen gab es
all diese Zeit her einen Glücklichen,
der vieler andrer Fehler mit sich trug,
was eine Last sein mußte, die ihn drückte,
nur daß ihn diese Drückerei beglückte.
Einstmals ging er im übrigen in einem
gewalt'gen Garten irgend etwas suchen.
Irgendwer gab ihm einen schwier'gen Auftrag,
den er kaum zu erled'gen hoffen durfte.
Auf dem Altan, das heißt, auf der Terrasse,
standen Gediegne, die ihn prüften, Herren
und Damen, eine prangende Versammlung,
aus der raketenähnlich ein Gelächter
stieg, und an diesem inhaltreichen Tage
zerbrach der dumme Bursche, der er war,
eine mit Malerein verzierte Tasse,
wonach mit einem Mal sich die Kulissen
verschoben. Immer blieb ihm manches Wicht'ge
fremd, er blieb töricht, doch um dieses Etwas
willen benied man ihn vielleicht mit Recht.
Stets schleppte er die Fehler vieler andrer
durchs Leben, und nach unten und nach oben
zog's ihn, er sah sich brauch- und unbrauchbar,
gelobt, getadelt und zerteilt und ganz.

THE LUCKY ONE

People have a gift for mouth and eye
and ear, and houses have doors, corridors,
windows, and in the alleys, in the halls there
was always a lucky one, who carried with him
the mistakes of others, what a burden
it must have been that pushed him down,
but he was pleased by all this pushing.
Once, by the way, he went to search
for something in a grand garden.
Someone had given him a difficult task
he couldn't possibly hope to complete.
Dignified men and women stood
on the Altan, the terrace, that is,
and scrutinized him, a splendid
gathering, from which, like rockets,
emerged laughter, and on this substantial day
the stupid boy that he was broke a hand
painted cup, whereupon at once the scenery
was shifted. There was always something
important that remained strange to him,
he remained foolish, but of this something
one was perhaps rightly envious. He always
hauled the mistakes of many others
through life, and he was being pulled down
and up, he saw himself useful and useless,
lauded, blamed and in pieces and whole.

ERZÄHLUNG

Mit einmal liebte ich sie nicht mehr,
oder ich bildete mir das nur ein,
oder dann war es so, daß ich es schön fand,
nicht mehr an sie zu denken.
Das Mädchen mit den Perlen hatte
zu mir gesprochen: «Du bist mein Gatte»,
obschon sie sich dabei durchaus nichts dachte
und ich es ihr wohl auch nicht glaubte, aber
ich war der ihrige; ging ich spazieren,
so tat ich's, weil ich sagte: «Sie erlaubt es mir.»
Hielt ich mich im Gemache auf,
geschah es wieder nur mit ihrem Willen.
Wie kam das, und wie kam es, daß auch sie mich
verlor und ich mit der Besitzerin
des Fächers den liebreizendsten
Vertrag einging, wonach ich nur vor ihr noch zittern,
mich nur um sie noch kümmern durfte?

STORY

Suddenly I no longer loved her,
or I just imagined it,
or it was that I found it nice
to no longer think of her.
The girl with the pearls had
spoken to me: "You are my husband,"
although she thought nothing of it
and I surely didn't believe her, but
I was hers; whenever I went on a walk,
I did it because I said: "She lets me."
When I was in the bedroom,
it happened only because of her.
How did it happen, and why did she lose me
too and I entered into the loveliest contract
with the owner of the fan, whereupon
I was allowed to shiver with fear,
to concern myself only with her?

DER FÜNFZIGSTE GEBURTSTAG

Geboren bin ich im April in einem
Städtchen mit reizender Umgebung, wo ich
zur Schule ging; Pfarrer und Lehrer waren
zum Teil mit mir zufrieden. Mit den Jahren
kam ich als Lehrling hübsch auf eine Bank,
wonach ich Städte sah wie Basel, Stuttgart
und Zürich. Hier macht' ich Bekanntschaft mit
einer gar gütigen und lieben Frau,
die bald die Stadt und bald die Landschaft, je,
wie es ihr förderlich erschien, bewohnte,
und die auf Heinrich Heine aufmerksam
mich machte, den ich sicher erst viel später
in seinem weiten Wert begreifen lernte.
Die Frau hieß, wie nur ich imstand wär', es
zu sagen, doch weswegen sollt' ich solches
tun, da mich Diskretion beglückt? Stellungen
in Handelshäusern hatt' ich manche inne.
Lebhaft verließ ich aus durchaus ureignem
Drang einen Platz, um einen neuen zu
erschwingen und versehen; nebenbei
schrieb ich im Industriequartier Gedichte,
die später im Verlag Bruno Cassirer
womöglich etwas zu pompös erschienen.
So gegen sieben Jahre lebte ich
dann in Berlin als ems'ger Prosaist
und kehrte, als die Herrn Verleger keinen

144

MY FIFTIETH BIRTHDAY

I was born in April in a small
town with a charming ambience,
where I went to school; pastors
and schoolmasters were sometimes
pleased with me. And in due course,
I became a proper bank apprentice,
whereupon I saw cities such as Basel,
Stuttgart and Zurich. This is where
I made the acquaintance of a most kind
and dear woman, who resided now in the city,
now in the country, according to which seemed
more favorable to her, and who drew my attention
to Heinrich Heine, whose great importance
I surely did not fully grasp until much later.
Only I could divulge the woman's name,
but why should I do so when discretion
pleases me? I held a good many positions
in trading houses. Cheerfully, and out of
an impulse entirely my own, I would leave
one post simply to afford and fill another;
on the side, I wrote poems in the industrial quarter
that later appeared, perhaps too pompously,
in the publishing firm Bruno Cassirer.
For about seven years I then lived
in Berlin as a hardworking prose writer
and, when the publishers were no longer

Vorschuß mir mehr gewähren wollten, in
die Schweiz zurück, die viele um der schönen
Berg' willen lieben, um hier unverdrossen
fernerhin dichterisch bemüht zu bleiben.

Nun zähl' ich immerhin schon fünfzig Jährchen,
sagen mir heute ein'ge graue Härchen.

willing to grant me an advance, I returned
to Switzerland, loved by so many people
for her beautiful mountains, to persist
undauntedly in my poetic efforts.
As it is I add up to a mere fifty years today,
I'm told by a few little gray hairs.

SIE LANGWEILTE SICH

Die Straßen waren ihr zu wenig fremd,
die Restaurants und Kinos kamen ihr
vor, so, als wollten sie ihr lästig fallen,
nicht müde war sie worden, nein, nur kalt,
eine Gleichgült'ge ging sie neben Menschen
und Wagen hin, Neues war nicht vorhanden,
die Herrenwelt zum Beispiel schien ihr alt,
junge und fröhl'che Leute machten ein
Gesicht, benahmen sich auf eine Weise,
daß sie den Gipfel der Unint'ressantheit
darstellten. Kokettieren lohnte sich
nicht mehr. «Langweilig ist mein Aufenthalt
in dieser einst für mich so hübschen Stadt
geworden», sprach sie zu sich selber. Täglich
dacht' sie dasselbe, wünschte sich genötigt,
zu reisen und doch liebt' sie das Verschmähte,
fand im Verachteten noch immer viel
Schönes, blieb nicht und ging nicht fort und sah sich
vertrieben und doch wieder angezogen
vom scheinbar schon zu lang Vertrauten,
fragend die Menschen ihr ins Antlitz schauten.

SHE WAS BORED

The streets were not strange enough
to her, the restaurants and cinemas
appeared as if they wanted to bother her,
she didn't grow tired, no, just cold,
an indifference, she walked beside people
and cars, there was nothing new, the world
of gentlemen, for example, seemed old,
young and happy people made a face,
behaved in such a way, they represented
the height of uninterestingness. Flirting
wasn't worth it anymore. "Bored is now
my stay in this city that was once
so beautiful to me," she told herself.
Every day she thought the same,
wished she were forced to travel,
yet she loved the despised, still
found much that was beautiful
in her scorn, didn't stay and didn't leave
and saw herself banished yet attracted
by that which had seemed familiar for too
long, questioning, the people faced her.

BESCHAULICHKEIT

Die Bücher waren alle schon geschrieben,
die Taten alle scheinbar schon getan.
Alles, was seine schönen Augen sahn,
stammte aus früherer Bemühung her.
Die Häuser, Brücken und die Eisenbahn
hatten etwas durchaus Bemerkenswertes.
Er dachte an den stürmischen Laertes,
an Lohengrin und seinen sanften Schwan,
und üb'rall war das Hohe schon getan,
stammte aus längstvergangnen Zeiten.
Man sah ihn einsam über Felder reiten.
Das Leben lag am Ufer wie ein Kahn,
der nicht mehr fähig ist zum Schaukeln, Gleiten.

CONTEMPLATION

All the books had already been written,
the deeds had seemingly all been done.
Everything his beautiful eyes saw
dated back to earlier efforts.
The houses, bridges and the railroad
had something quite remarkable about them.
He thought of the impetuous Laertes,
of Lohengrin and his gentle swan,
and everywhere great art had already
been achieved in times long past.
You saw him ride lonely across the fields.
Life lay by the riverside like a boat
no longer able to sway, to drift.

AFTERWORD

On 8 May 1898, *Der Bund* (the Sunday newspaper of the *Berner Tageszeitung*) published six short, unsigned poems, with an introduction by the paper's literary editor, Josef Viktor Widman, who titled the selection, "Lyric Firstlings." Widman, at the time Switzerland's most respected literary critic, had selected the six short pieces from a notebook of forty poems. In his introduction, Widman explains that he was "immensely attracted by [the poems'] truly new sounds," and, aside from pointing to a few minor stylistic shortcomings, declares his "respect for a natural talent that, despite all obstacles, often safely knows how to find true and unusual words for true and unusual emotions." That selection, as far as we know, represents the first published work of Robert Walser's, then a twenty-year-old clerk working in Zurich.

In "Das erste Gedicht" (The First Poem) and "Die Gedichte" (Poems) (*Sämtliche Werke* 6: 252 and 254) (hereinafter referred to as *SW*), Walser writes about the origins of his early poems. "I don't really know how I came to poetry," he says in the latter. "I was reading poems, and then it occurred to me that I should write some of my own. It happened like anything else. I've often asked myself how it all began. Well, it caught me by the tail and carried me away. I didn't know what I was doing. I was writing poems from a mixture of bright-golden prospects and worried hopelessness, always half in fear and half in an almost overflowing elation." A brief profile published in the *Leserzirkel* in November 1920 confirms that Walser was writing poems during his time in Zurich and that "he didn't do so on the side but rather, in the belief that art required absolute devotion, 'made himself unemployed' in order to write" (*SW* 20: 433).

In the summer of 1898, Walser met his second supporter, the Austrian Franz Blei, who had read Walser's poems in *Der Bund*. Walser's prose piece "Doktor Franz Blei" (*SW* 5: 212) clearly shows the influence this sophisticated critic and essayist had on the young poet. Blei found Walser's poems "true and proper, from the inside. Nowhere does rhyme tower over meaning. Not one of the poems is modulated by a melody that overpowers the ear. Poetry is not a sacrifice to music, nor language to rhythm, or words to melos. There is nothing that could go beyond the experiences of a seventeen-year-old boy. With a certain Swiss stubbornness, this young poet, unafraid of the consequences, remains true to the localities of his life . . ." ("Zeitgenossen," *Der kleine Bund*, 10 October 1937).

It is clear that Blei, who introduced Walser to Goethe, Lenz, Büchner, and Brentano, was unaware of the young poet's actual age; he even backdated the "seventeen-year-old's" poems published in his journal *Der Lose Vogel* to 1893. (Walser would have been fifteen or sixteen at the time, living with his parents in Biel, and working as an apprentice at the local Kantonalbank.) It was, in fact, 1897 when the then nineteen-year-old Walser began writing poems. Compared to those first published in *Der Bund*, and the unpublished selection Blei read in Walser's notebooks, however, they seem rather unoriginal and self-sentimentally ecstatic. The young Walser certainly knew that his uncontrolled outpouring of emotions and words, the common connections between traditional forms and truisms, would not lead to an authentic voice. He had other things to say, and he found the means to do so by turning back to what he knew best. Perhaps, as he says in "Das erste Gedicht," the beginning was really the wintry

"Ein Landschäftchen" (A Little Landscape), one of the "firstlings" published in *Der Bund* in May 1898.

"Ein Landschäftchen" was one of the forty poems in the notebook Walser had originally sent to Widman. Franz Blei, whom Walser visited twice in Zurich, once in the summer of 1898 and then again in the spring of 1899, remembered another notebook with roughly twenty poems that Walser had given to him ("one more beautiful than the other," he wrote to Otto Julius Bierbaum). In 1972, a notebook with the title "Drittes Buch. Saite und Sehnsucht" (Third Book. String and Desire) surfaced from the collected papers of Walser's youngest sister, Fanny, in which Walser had written close to fifty poems. The handwriting points to early 1899 or 1900, certainly one of Walser's most prolific and fruitful periods of literary production, though many of the texts from that period, mostly handwritten copies sent to friends and editors, have been lost or destroyed. Unfortunately, the chronological relationship between the various notebooks, and whether or not their contents overlapped, cannot be established. We can assume, however, that most, if not all, of the early poems (published up until 1913) were first written between 1898 and 1900.

Blei eventually introduced Walser to Otto Julius Bierbaum, Alfred Walter Heymel, and Rudolf Alexander Schröder, the founding editors of the Munich-based magazine *Die Insel*. The fact that Walser published several poems and essays, as well as four dramatic pieces, in the first three volumes of this prestigious magazine would have certainly encouraged his artistic ambitions. In 1904, Heymel's Insel Verlag published Walser's first book, *Fritz Kocher's Aufsätze* (Fritz Kocher's Essays), but several years of sluggish negotiations meant that Walser's efforts to publish both a collection of poems and a book of dramatic pieces were fruitless. It must be said, however, that Heymel was quite supportive of Walser's work, unlike Insel's director of publishing, Anton Kippenberger. In addition to the magazine *Die Insel*, Walser's poems appeared in Blei's *Die Opale*, the weekly journal *Der Samstag*, the Berlin-based *Schaubühne*, and Julius Zeitler's *Deutscher Almanach auf das Jahr 1907*. In 1905/06, Walser settled in

Berlin and dedicated most of his time to the writing of prose. Only after the publication of two novels with Bruno Cassirer did Walser decide, again, to publish a collection of poems. It appeared in 1909, "perhaps too pompously," as he says in "My Fiftieth Birthday," as a limited-edition quarto (300 copies), 38 pages long, with 16 fine etchings by Walser's brother, Karl, printed on real Bütten paper. The subscription price was set at thirty marks.

Widman published a kind and respectful review of Walser's collection (he found, with only a few exceptions, the same poems he had read in the notebook in 1898) in the *Sonntagsblatt* (21 March 1909). In essence, the collection serves as a showcase of the majority of poems Walser had published over the previous ten years. Bierbaum also wrote a review, for the Vienna-based *Zeit* (11 April 1909), in which he compares Walser to Verlaine, and confirms the mixed reviews Walser's collection had received: " When I point to Walser's poems (with only a few words, for how much can one say when one is filled with astonishment?), allow me to remind you that Walser is one of the poets whose work first appeared in *Die Insel*, one of the poets whose work contributed to the fact that many believed *Die Insel* was not worthy of serious attention. One of the poems even found its way into the national papers: as a symptom of modern idiocy . . . today the danger might be quite the opposite: Walser as an object of snobbish rapture." Bierbaum praised Walser's "uniqueness, which is completely authentic": "We simply do not have another lyric poet like Walser (except for Dauthendey, perhaps), and one who is such a confident (somnambulistically so) artist of the word." Aside from those two reviews, however, the late and expensive publication of Walser's collection failed to attract much attention. Walser's distinctive voice, subtle and delicate, was finally not enough to be seen as something sensationally novel.

Only two further poems appeared between 1908 and 1918, published by Max Brod in *Arkadia*—"Handharfe am Tag" (Lyre by Day) (1913) and the motto for "Kleine Dichtungen" (Short Poems) (1914)—both in the style of Walser's early poems. During his time in Biel (1913 to 1920), much, if not all, of Walser's lyricism found a home in his predominantly nature-inspired prose.

In 1919, Bruno Cassirer published a second—and much cheaper—edition of Walser's *Poems*. In the midst of all the postwar turmoil and in the vicinity of a rather noisy neighborhood called "expressionism," however, Walser's collection again failed to attract much attention. In a review in the *Berner Bund* (1920), Otto von Greyerz calls the poems Widman had praised in 1909, "lifeless" and "decadent." Hans Bethge, on the other hand, published an essay on the Brothers Walser in the *Kleine Bund* (1920), in which he writes: "We are looking at lovely, inward-looking, and frequently quite ironic poems that are dreamy and spellbinding. In fact, these tender and delicate poems possess an inner form and radiance."

The year 1919 was not only significant in terms of the publication of the second edition of *Poems* but also because Walser entered a second period of lyric production. The poems Walser wrote and published between 1919 and 1920 are considerably different compared to his earlier work: they are relatively long, they do not rhyme, and, like most of the late poems, they use a colloquial, almost chatty, language similar to—if not more pronounced than—Walser's simple and relaxed prose he wrote during his time in Biel. They lack, however, the problematic questioning and encrypted symbolism found in the poems of Walser's third period.

Walser acknowledges the discontinuity of his lyric production in "Meine Bemühungen" (My Efforts) (*SW* 20: 427): "When I was twenty, I wrote poems, and when I was forty-eight, I began to write new poems." Yet Walser's statement cannot be taken literally, for it is problematic not only in regards to the small number of poems he wrote in Berlin and Biel but, more importantly, in regards to the year 1926, the beginning of Walser's late period in Berne. Walser's new work appeared in newspapers and journals in 1925, and the first drafts of "Mikrogramme" (Microscripts), found in the *Nachlass* and edited by Bernhard Echte and Werner Morlang, point to the summer of 1924. In 1921, after almost eight years in Biel, Walser arrived in Berne, where, as a forty-two-year old, he worked briefly as a librarian at the Berner Staatsarchiv. Walser faced extreme financial hardship in Berne, but he was saved twice by a modest inheritance, which might account for the fact that his literary production was minimal until the beginning of 1924 (though he did write a short novel, *Theodor*, in 1921). Nevertheless, 1924 marked the beginning of an extraordinary three-year period of literary production for Walser, which included the stories published in 1925 in *Die Rose* (The Rose), Walser's last published book. Walser developed his "late style" in those stories, in which he blends, often ludically, fiction, essays, and reportage, and combines the most disparate motifs, cryptograms, and reflections; his texts turned into experimental language fields, where the trivial meets the original (sometimes generating rather grotesque effects).

The daily stream of prose also included new poems, some inspired perhaps by a mysterious romantic episode he writes about in his various "Edith" texts (in *Die Rose* or in *The Robber*, for example). Not much is known about this episode, yet we can sense that it had a lasting effect on Walser, and many of the poems reflect on this platonic/Petrarchan relationship. The various objects of everyday life, the experience of nature, self-reflection, as well as social, literary, and historic motifs, served as further inspiration for new poems. Walser continued to write poems until June 1933, the year he entered—against his will—the sanatorium in Herisau. In fact, according to Walser, during the three-and-a-half years he spent in the Waldau asylum (Walser suffered a mental breakdown in 1929), he often wrote more poetry than prose: "Among other things, I kept a kind of diary in the form of individual poems, separate and completely independent of each other" (from a letter to his friend Frieda Mermet, 23 December 1929). And on 10 June 1930, he told Therese Breitbach that "in here I've written over one hundred new poems." After decades of focusing mostly on prose, Walser the poet can certainly be seen as somewhat of a late bloomer.

The word "lyric" often implies a sophisticated sense of language and an extraordinary state of mind. Most of Walser's late poems can therefore not be called "lyric," and Franz Blei's comments on Walser's early poems would better fit the late work. They are often simple prose pieces, where only the surface properties are reminiscent of a poem; many do not use rhyme and employ metrical irregularities. (In an early draft for the *Microscripts*, we can see that Walser's story "Das Bäumchen" [The Small Tree] was actually first written as a poem, which serves as further proof of Walser's arbitrary fashion of determining a text's form and genre). Walser's use of strange inversions, and the absence of vowels in certain words, for example, often feels very odd and clumsy—much like an amateur poet's work. Every so often we are reminded of the poems by Friederike Kempner or Mary Stirnemann-Zysset. But Walser knew the common standards. Considering Walser's removal of poetic tension, we can assume that Walser was very deliberately creating poems in complete diametrical opposition to the highly refined and in some cases esoteric poems written by his contemporaries, such as George, Rilke, Hofmannstahl, Schröder, and Hesse. The critical and ironic interpretation of literature we encounter in Walser's poems, letters, and conversations (see Carl Seelig's *Wanderungen mit Robert Walser* [Walks with Robert Walser], Frankfurt a. M., 1977) make it probable that Walser was motivated by a "countermove" against the "significant" and "perfectly structured." Meanwhile, between the banal and the bizarre, we find, again and again, poetic beauty and illuminating aperçus, values not associated with true dilettantism, as well as a very original, albeit cryptic, sense of humor. We should not psychologize and dismiss Walser's work as a poet because he occasionally embarrasses us; similarly, we should not simply dismiss the sometimes provocative and strange features of Walser's late prose as pathological. It is problematic to speak of an illness or medical condition when discussing Walser's writing, for the nature, cause, and circumstances of Walser's precarious state of mind that led to his institutionalization have yet to be fully clarified.

Walser knew exactly what he was doing. In a letter to Max Rychner (18 March 1926), he confirms not only the above-mentioned assumption but offers the reader a glimpse of his poetics: "I find Kerr's question about whether a certain degree of stupidity is required in the writing of poems remarkable . . . There is something bright and beautiful and good in the notion of stupidity, something ineffably valuable and delicate, something the most intelligent have yearned for and tried to make their own . . . In all forms of poetry, the intellect is 'only' a servant, and the poet whose servant listens properly, that is, listens in terms of the artist's needs, writes at his best, and Kerr's question concerning stupidity ought to be translated in terms of the servant's usefulness and suppleness . . . The poem arises from the intellectual's desire to relinquish a large portion of his intellect." While Walser's prose pieces are already spontaneous creations, "out of knowledge and ignorance," his poems are received fruits of an artistic self-indulgence, with rhyme and meter being external rather than internal vehicles. In one of his many conversations with Carl Seelig, Walser further discusses his idyllicized and "simple" poems: "If I could begin again, I would try to systematically eliminate the subjective and write for the good of the people" (*Wanderungen mit Robert Walser* 78).

Walser's financial situation during his years in Berne, however, would not have encouraged this kind of writing; Walser's living expenses increased drastically (his stay at the Waldau sanatorium being the main cause), and he often had to rely on the support of his siblings. It is due solely to the sympathy and goodwill of Otto Pick and Max Brod that Walser saw the publication of a number of new poems. Between 1925 and 1933, Pick published over eighty poems in the *Prager Presse*, and between 1925 and 1931, Brod, against the will of the newspaper's chief editor, published over thirty poems, as well as a few prose pieces, in the *Prager Tagblatt*.

A bibliographic note on three of Walser's poems published in *Saat und Ernte* (1925), an anthology edited by Albrecht Sergel, mentions a new collection of poems, *New Poems*, apparently being prepared by the Ernst Rowohlt Verlag. This would have been a surprisingly early plan for a new collection; it seems more likely that Walser was actually referring to *The Rose*. Unfortunately, Walser did not see another published collection of his poems during the last three decades of his life. In 1927, Max Brod failed to convince the editors at Paul Zsolnay Verlag in Vienna to publish a collection of Walser's new poems. In a letter to Pick (5 October 1927), however, Walser sees "no rush." Carl Seelig edited a collection of Walser's late poems, *Unbekannte Gedichte* (Unknown Poems), which was published by Verlag Tschudy in 1958, two year's after Walser's death.

REFERENCES

Im Bureau / *In the Office* (1897/98). From *Gedichte* (Poems) (1909). First published in *Die Opale* (1907).

Wintersonne / *Winter Sun*. From *Gedichte* (1909). First published in *Die Opale* (1907). The original version is divided into two six-line stanzas and serves as the "opening poem" for a selection Walser compiled for *Die Opale*. Walser prefaced the selection, which includes a total of eight poems, with the following "motto": "That's what I call a silent night, / a night that doesn't mind its stars."

Warum auch? / *But Why?* From *Gedichte* (1909). First published in *Die Opale* (1907). In the original version, the last two lines read, "something must, yes, something must / happen—then a consideration caught up with him."

Die Bäume / *The Trees* (1899/1900). From *Gedichte* (1909).

Brausen / *Rushing*. From *Gedichte* (1909). First published as *Kein Halt* (No End) in *Die Opale* (1907).

Wie immer / *As Always*. From *Gedichte* (1909). First published as *Kein Ausweg* (No Escape) in *Der Bund* (8 May 1898).

Schäferstunde / Tryst. From *Gedichte* (1909). First published in *Die Opale* (1907). The original version is divided into five four-line stanzas.

Weiter / Onwards (1899/1900). From *Gedichte* (1909). Published as *Always Onwards* in *Saite und Sehnsucht* (String and Desire) (1979).

Sünde / Sin (1899/1900). From *Gedichte* (1909).

Ein Landschäftchen / A Little Landscape. From *Gedichte* (1909). First published in *Der Bund* (8 May 1898).

Beiseit / Put Aside. From *Gedichte* (1909). First published as *Saying* (with "freed" as the last word of the poem) in *Wiener Rundschau* (1 August 1899).

Drückendes Licht / Oppressive Light. From *Gedichte* (1909). First published as *Poem* in *Freistatt* (17 December 1904).

Bangen / Afraid. From *Gedichte* (1909). First published in *Wiener Rundschau* (1 August 1899) and reprinted in *Die Opale* (1907) and Julius Zeitler's *Deutscher Almanach auf das Jahr 1907* (1907).

Und ging / And Left. From *Gedichte* (1909). First published in *Wiener Rundschau* (1 August 1899).

Stunde / Hour. From *Gedichte* (1909). First published in *Die Insel* (June 1900).

Trüber Nachbar / Gloomy Neighbor. From *Saite und Sehnsucht* (1979). First published in *Der Bund* (8 May 1898).

Feierabend / Closing Time (1898). From a letter written by Franz

Mutlos / Taint-Heurted. From *Saite und Sehnsucht* (1979). First
published in Julius Zeitler's *Deutscher Almanach auf das Jahr 1907*
(1907).

Trauerspiel / Tragedy. From *Saite und Sehnsucht* (1979). First
published in *Die Schaubühne* (April 1907).

Frühling / Spring. First published in *Pro Helvetia* (May 1919).

Oktober / October. First published in *Schweizerisches
Familienwochenblatt* (October 1920).

Nach Zeichnungen von Daumier / After Drawings by Daumier. Only
the drawings described in the last two stanzas have been identified.
The "man in the pleasure boat" is based on Number 16, "Une recontre
désagréable," in the series of lithographed drawings titled "Les
canotiers Parisiens," first published in *Charivari* on 6 July 1843 (no.
1038 in Loys Delteil's catalogue *Honoré Daumier*, Paris, 1925/26).
The gentleman in the barbershop is based on Number 22 in the series
titled "Mœurs conjugales," first published in *Charivari* on 5 April 1840
(no. 645 in Delteil), with the following note: "C'est ma femme!! oh!
scélérate, pendant qu'on me fait la barbe, elle me fait la queue!" The
first stanza is probably based on the woodcut "Le Poète de salon,"
pg. 85, *Physiologie du poète*, Sylvius, Paris, 1841 (no. 306 in Arthur
Rümann's catalogue *Honoré Daumier / Sein Holzschnittwerk*, Munich,
1914). First published in *Kunst und Künstler* (November 1920).

Wie die Hügelchen lächelten / How the Small Hills Smiled. First
published in *Wissen und Leben* (June 1925) and then reprinted in
Albert Segel's anthology *Saat und Ernte* (1925).

Sonntagvormittägliche Fahnen / *Sunday Morning Flags* (1925). First published in *Prager Presse* (May 1928).

Empfindung / *Sensation* (1926/27). First published in *Prager Tagblatt* (October 1927).

Die Jahreszeiten / *The Seasons* (1927). First published in *Prager Tagblatt* (November 1927).

Wie ich ein Blatt fallen sah / *How I Saw a Leaf Falling.* First published in *Prager Tagblatt* (October 1927).

Festzug / *Parade* (1927). From a letter to Otto Pick, 17 September 1927: "Here's 'Parade,' a poem I wrote to celebrate the occasion of the Bernese costume festival two weeks ago, trying to give it a sense of general importance." First published in *Prager Presse* (August 1933).

Das Sehnen / *Longing.* First published in *Prager Tagblatt* (June 1928).

Herbst (II) / *Autumn (II).* First published in *Prager Tagblatt* (October 1930).

Der Leser / *The Reader* (1930). Unpublished.

Lebensfreude / *Joy of Life* (1930). Unpublished.

Sommer / *Summer* (1931). First published in *Prager Presse* (September 1931).

Annehmlichkeit des Klagens / *The Comfort of Complaining* (1930). Walser originally titled this poem "The Comfort of Forgetting." Unpublished.

Schlaf / *Sleep* (1930). Unpublished.

Das Schöne / *The Beautiful* (1930). Unpublished.

Hohe Schule / *High Art* (1930). The first performance of *Falstaff*, Verdi's last opera, took place on 9 February 1893 at La Scala in Milan. First published in *Prager Presse* (March 1930).

Das Sonett vom Zuchthaus / *The Jail Sonnet*. First published in *Prager Presse* (May 1927).

Rätsel / *Riddles* (1926/27). First published in *Neue Schweizer Rundschau* (September 1927).

Die Dame im Reitkleid / *Lady in Riding Habit*. Langenthal is an industrial town in the canton of Berne. The "Lady of Langenthal," however, seems to be a fictitious figure. First published in *Simplicissimus* (June 1925).

Das Mädchen mit den schönen Augen / *The Girl with the Beautiful Eyes*. First published in *Prager Presse* (February 1926).

An Georg Trakl / *To Georg Trakl*. First published in *Prager Presse* (February 1928).

Der Gefährte / *The Companion* (1927/28). From a letter to Otto Pick (which included two poems—"Der Gefährte" and "Der Revolutionär"): ". . . Mister Werfel served as the model for my companion. . . ." This is the only known record of a meeting between Walser and Franz Werfel. First published in *Prager Presse* (April 1928).

Selbstschau / *Self-Reflection* (1925). First published in *Prager Presse* (February 1933).

Der Archivar / The Archivist (1930). In 1921, Walser was an assistant archivist at the Public Record Office of the Canton of Berne. Unpublished.

Glosse / Gloss. From 1888 until 1892, Walser attended the Progymnasium der Stadt Biel, which was founded as a secondary school or Collège in 1803, when Biel belonged to France. First published in *Neue Schweizer Rundschau* (July 1927).

Der Glückliche / The Lucky One (1928/29). First published in *Prager Presse* (April 1933).

Erzählung / Story. First published in *Prager Tagblatt* (November 1927).

Der fünfzigste Geburtstag / My Fiftieth Birthday (1928). The poem's unnamed woman, Walser's female friend from Zurich, also appears in Walser's short story "Luise" and, as Klara, in the novels *Der Gehülfe* (The Assistant) (1908) and *Geschwister Tanner* (The Tanners) (1907).

Sie langweilte sich / She Was Bored (1930). Unpublished.

Beschaulichkeit / Contemplation (1930). Unpublished.

ABOUT THE AUTHOR

Robert Walser (1878-1956) was born in Switzerland. He left school at fourteen and led a wandering and precarious existence while producing poems, stories, essays, and three novels: *The Tanners* (1906), *The Assistant* (1908), and *Jakob Von Gunten* (1909). In 1933, he abandoned writing and entered a sanatorium, where he remained for the rest of his life. "I am not here to write," Walser said, "but to be mad."

ABOUT THE TRANSLATOR

Daniele Pantano is a Swiss poet, translator, critic, and editor born of Sicilian and German parentage in Langenthal (Canton of Berne). His individual poems, essays, and reviews, as well as his translations from the German by Friedrich Dürrenmatt, Georg Trakl, and Robert Walser, have appeared or are forthcoming in numerous magazines, journals, and anthologies worldwide. Pantano's most recent works include *In an Abandoned Room: Selected Poems by Georg Trakl* (Erbacce Press, 2008), *The Possible Is Monstrous: Selected Poems by Friedrich Dürrenmatt* and *The Oldest Hands in the World* (both from Black Lawrence Press/Dzanc Books, 2010), and *Mass Graves (XIX-XXII)* (The Knives, Forks and Spoons Press, 2011). Pantano has taught at the University of South Florida and served as the Visiting Poet-in-Residence at Florida Southern College. He divides his time between Switzerland, the United States, and England, where he is Senior Lecturer and Director of Creative Writing at Edge Hill University. For more information, please visit www.danielepantano.ch.

ACKNOWLEDGMENTS

I wish to thank Diane Goettel, my wonderful editor at Black Lawrence Press, for her enthusiasm and encouragement, and the editors of the following journals, in which some of these translations first appeared: *The Adirondack Review*, *Erbacce Magazine*, *Mayday Magazine*, and *Guernica Magazine*. My thanks to Petra Hardt, Nora Mercurio, and Richard Stoiber at Suhrkamp, and to Reto Sorg at the Robert Walser Zentrum. And Matthew Lewis for another brilliant cover image. I am very indebted to friends and colleagues for their support: Billy Collins, Okla Elliott, Carolyn Forché, Jay Hopler, and Victor Peppard. And I am also grateful to Edge Hill University for financial support during the writing of this book. Endless gratitude to James Reidel for his friendship, inspiration, and guidance. Last, and most important, I thank my parents, Giuseppe and Katharina, my brother, Michel, my beautiful children, Fiona and Giacomo, and my beautiful and talented wife, Nicole, for their unceasing love, support, and inspiration.

INDEX OF TITLES AND FIRST LINES IN ENGLISH

Page numbers refer to the text; those in italics, following poem titles, point to the references.

INDEX OF TITLES AND FIRST LINES IN GERMAN

Page numbers refer to the text; those in italics, following poem titles, point to the references.